THE QUOTATIONS OF
CHAIRMAN
GREENSPAN

# Other Books by Larry Kahaner

## Nonfiction

*Competitive Intelligence: How to Gather, Analyze, and Use Information to Move Your Business to the Top*

*Say It and Live It: The 50 Corporate Mission Statements That Hit the Mark* (coauthor)

*Cults That Kill: Probing the Underworld of Occult Crime*

*On the Line: The Men of MCI Who Took on AT&T and Won*

## Fiction

*Naked Prey* (under the pseudonym Larry Kane)

## Forthcoming

*The Talmud Way of Business: Ancient Lessons About Ethics and Profits for Today's Business Professionals*

# THE QUOTATIONS OF CHAIRMAN GREENSPAN

## Words from the Man Who Can Shake the World

**Larry Kahaner**

Adams Media Corporation
Holbrook, Massachusetts

Published by
Adams Media Corporation
260 Center Street, Holbrook, MA 02343
www.adamsmedia.com

ISBN: 1-58062-420-0

Printed in Canada.

J I H G F E D C B

Library of Congress Cataloging-in-Publication Data
available from the publisher.

This publication is designed to provide accurate and authoritative information with
regard to the subject matter covered. It is sold with the understanding that the publisher is not engaged in rendering legal, accounting, or other professional advice. If
legal advice or other expert assistance is required, the services of a competent professional person should be sought.
　　　—From a *Declaration of Principles* jointly adopted by a Committee of the
American Bar Association and a Committee of Publishers and Associations.

Cover photo by Brad Markell/Liason Agency

*This book is available at quantity discounts for bulk purchases.*
*For information, call 1-800-872-5627.*

**Visit our exciting small business Web site: www.businesstown.com**

# Contents

Federal Reserve chairman Alan Greenspan is extremely cautious with his words. Even the most innocent comment from him can send shockwaves through financial markets. While attending a Kennedy Center affair, he ran into Securities and Exchange Commission chairman Arthur Levitt.

"How are you, Alan?" asked Levitt.

"I'm not allowed to say," Greenspan joked.

# Introduction

# Who Is Alan Greenspan, and Why Has He Been So Successful?

**W**ho would have thought that an economist could become a superstar on a par with the world's most popular movie stars or rock idols?

Meet Alan Greenspan, a 74-year-old bespectacled, somewhat owlish looking man who has been called the second most powerful man in Washington. Which, if you do the quick math, makes him the second most powerful person in the world.

But unlike a slick, outrageous celebrity gracing the cover of *Rolling Stone,* Greenspan is demure, even modest about his work and achievements. Respected by those close to him for his honesty, thoughtfulness, and kindness, he toils in the unglamorous field of economics.

So what is it about this man that has made him so potent that a few carefully chosen words from him can sink markets—or raise them? Why do statesmen around the world, regardless of their political conviction, seek his counsel? Why does Congress, arguably the mightiest political institution in human history, hang on his every statement in awe of his financial acumen?

How has this soft-spoken mystery man remained largely inaccessible to the public at large but at the same time free of political strings and partisan obligations?

Who is this rock-steady man who touches our daily lives, guiding this country through uncharted economic waters, leading us to the greatest prosperity the world has ever seen?

Just who is Alan Greenspan?

# The Early Years

Alan Greenspan was born on March 6, 1926, in the Washington Heights section of New York City. His father, Herbert, was a stockbroker who divorced his wife, Rose, when Alan was a boy. He attended George Washington High School (along with Henry Kissinger) and showed a flair for music and mathematics.

After high school, Greenspan studied music at the Julliard School, where his facility with the saxophone and clarinet earned him a spot in a swing band. Not interested in pursuing a music career, he enrolled in New York University at 19 as an economics major. He graduated summa cum laude in 1948 with a Bachelor of Science degree. He went on to receive his master's degree from NYU, then went to Columbia for postgraduate study. While at Columbia, he became friends with Arthur Burns, who was later to become chairman of the Council of Economic Advisors under President Eisenhower and, later still, chairman of the Federal Reserve from 1970 through 1978. While at Columbia, Greenspan married his first wife, painter Joan Mitchell.

It was around this time that Greenspan became enamored with the works of Ayn Rand, author of the popular book *Atlas Shrugged*. He would meet with others at Rand's home for discussion circles. These roundtables led Greenspan to develop his thoughts about economic systems that highlighted the "morality" of capitalism—because it did the most good for the most people—individual responsibility, and a laissez-faire attitude of government toward business in general. These were tenets of Rand and her followers.

Now 28 years old, his marriage annulled, and short on money, Greenspan dropped out of the PhD program to become a professional economist. Along with bond trader William Townsend, he established Townsend-Greenspan &

Co. (Greenspan took the consultancy over when Townsend died in 1958) and built it into a premier economic forecasting consultancy whose clients included *Fortune* 500 companies. Until 1987, when Greenspan dissolved the business to focus on his career at the Federal Reserve, he had built an impeccable, unshakable reputation as a skilled forecaster.

# In Government Service

Greenspan got his first taste of government work when he became director of policy research for Richard Nixon's campaign in 1968. Later, he worked as an advisor to the president's transition team. He went back to private practice until 1974, when he was asked to head the president's Council of Economic Advisors. At first he refused the offer—Greenspan didn't like Nixon—but was persuaded by his old friend Arthur Burns, who was then Fed chairman. When Nixon resigned in August, President Ford extended the offer and he took the job, which ended in 1977. Once again, he returned to Townsend-Greenspan but now found that his years in Washington—he had received some credit for the economy's improvement—had given him celebrity status. He was being asked his views on television and other media and even did a TV ad for Apple Computer. He played a venerable financial advisor; it was not a stretch.

From 1981 to 1983, Greenspan chaired the bipartisan National Commission on Social Security Reform at a time when concerns about the program's future were beginning to be raised. The position was considered political quicksand as each side dug in its heels based on ideology. To his credit, and to the surprise of many, Greenspan pushed reforms through Congress while keeping the White House and lawmakers happy at the same time. Greenspan's political star was rising and shining brightly.

# At the Fed

The Federal Reserve was established in 1913 to oversee the economy. The chairman actually has two jobs. He is the head of the board of governors, made up of himself and six other appointed officials. The chairman also oversees the Federal Open Market Committee (FOMC), composed of the seven Fed governors and the heads of the 12 regional Federal Reserve banks (five of whom vote at any given time). The FOMC is the body that votes to raise or lower interest rates. The chairman does not have the final decision. He has only one vote, but his views are considered most important.

In 1987, Paul Volcker's chairmanship as Federal Reserve chairman was ending, and it become clear that President Reagan was not going to reappoint him. Volcker was in continual conflict with the administration over his method of taming inflation, which was to raise interest rates even though that slowed down the economy. Volcker was a hero, but not to administration Republicans, who were "supply-siders."

It is useful to consider how Greenspan and Volcker were so different from the economists who came before them. During the first half of the twentieth century, the ideas of the British economist John Maynard Keynes were gospel. Among other theories, he held that high unemployment was a result of insufficient consumer spending and that it could be relieved by more government spending. He added that the government should stimulate the economy even if it meant spending money it didn't have—deficit spending. Keynes's theories gained great popularity because government spending pulled the United States and many other countries out of the Great Depression of the 1930s. One practical downside, however, was that if employment was at too high a level, you could bring on inflation because fully employed workers spend lots of money and drive the prices of goods and services higher.

In the 1950s, a group of economists championed by Nobel laureate Milton Friedman believed that Keynes was off-base. They were known as "monetarists" because they believed that money supply drove the economy. By manipulating the amount of money in circulation, they could push and pull the economy to stimulate or contract economic growth. This was a radical departure because it meant that, in theory at least, we could have full employment and low inflation. We could have economic growth, high consumer demand, and stable prices all at the same time. These economists also believed that government was not the best judge of how the economy should operate; the marketplace itself was. Most important, government intervention, especially spending, should be at a minimum, and deficit spending was an absolute no-no.

Much of this remained theory until Volcker took office and, by using the Fed's power to control the money supply, got inflation under control through monetary practices, mainly the raising or lowering of interest rates. The Republican administration didn't cotton to Democrat Volcker when his monetarist policies, which were in conflict with its supply/demand beliefs, whipped inflation. They were jealous of his success. In fairness, they complained that monetary policy temporarily slows down growth, sometimes making borrowing money expensive (because of high interest rates) and that Volcker's practices caused a lot of business failures along the way. True, but to Volcker and other monetarists this was the short-term cost of a long-term solution. Monetarist policy is akin to the old saw about breaking eggs to make an omelet. In Volcker's case, his policy stopped inflation, but the price was a hefty 10 percent unemployment rate and a massive recession in the short term.

When Volcker's tenure was up, he and the Administration had just about had it with each other, and Greenspan's name was on the short list as a replacement. Even though he was a monetarist, which even now many Republicans were willing to admit worked, at least Greenspan was a Republican. He had no experience as a central banker, but he was hailed as a superb forecaster and a person of high integrity.

Once in office, Greenspan continued Volcker's legacy, applying what's called the Fed's "levers of power" to the economy to stimulate long-term growth and price stability—another phrase for low inflation. The three levers that the Fed has at its disposal are (1) open market operations; the buying and selling of Treasury bonds, (2) setting the reserve requirements of banks; how much they need to hold in cash reserves, and (3) setting interest rates charged to banks; this determines how much it costs banks to borrow money so they can lend it to their customers.

As you can see, the Fed, through these three levers, controls how much money is in circulation. By money, we mean hard cash, money in bank accounts, CDs, money market funds, and so on. All of these tools work to control the money supply, but the most well known tool is the Fed's control of interest rates, including the "discount rate" at which it lends money to banks. If the discount rate goes up, lending by banks goes down, and the growth of the money supply slows down. The Fed makes policy changes in interest rates at infrequent intervals, usually in increments of 0.25 percent, also called "25 basis points." Treasury bill rates, the prime lending rate, and savings account rates all tend to move together with this change.

How does the stock market react to these levers? Let's say the Fed "tightens the money supply" by increasing the interest rate. Although the whole process is a bit more complicated than I'm showing here, the upshot is that there is less money available for people to borrow and buy stocks. Now, when we say "less money" we really mean that, yes, the actual amount of money in circulation is lessened and, because of supply and demand, what's left is more expensive to get hold of. These, then, are the basics of monetarism as practiced by Greenspan.

Greenspan is a macroeconomist, meaning that he looks at the big picture yet understands the underlying factors. Former U.S. Representative Frank Ikard (D–Texas) once said of Greenspan: "He is the kind of person who knows how many thousands of flat-headed bolts were used in a Chevrolet and what it would do to the national economy if you took out three of them."

During his 13 years as Fed chairman, Greenspan has faced many challenges. While in office only a few months, he was confronted with a severe stock market crash on October 19, 1987. He reacted coolly and calmly, pumping money into the economy slowly to help rebuild lost confidence. It worked and the market recovered.

Over the years, the Fed was compelled to raise interest rates on many occasions even though there was no overt evidence of inflation. To Greenspan, these were "preemptive" strikes designed to head off inflation. He has been criticized for raising rates without visible inflationary signals, but in the end his fine tuning has proven correct. To Greenspan, the economy is a like a machine with a million little gears that must be oiled, cajoled, and tweaked for optimum performance. If any single gear is acting odd, it must be taken care of before it affects those around it.

During the last recession, from mid-1990 to March 1991, Greenspan stuck to his belief that a recovery was near and refused to raise interest rates. He was chastised for not doing anything to rejuvenate the economy quickly, but he was correct in his assertion on this account as well. The recovery did appear and again his forecast was on the money.

Since that recession, the Fed has met the twin goals of maximum employment and stable prices, a condition that economists for decades believed was impossible. This fact alone has earned Greenspan his place as the world's master central banker.

On the private side, we know little about Greenspan's life except that he and his wife, NBC correspondent Andrea Mitchell (they married in April 1997; he was 71, she was 50, and the 75 guests were a who's who of Washington), are fixtures in Washington's social circles. Friends say that Greenspan is kind and gentle. His marriage toast to his wife was "I intend to make her happy—and I will succeed."

We know that Greenspan is prone to take long hot baths in the morning, where it is said he does much of his thinking about the economy. He writes his speeches in longhand and is an avid tennis player.

His salary is about $140,000 annually, many times less than that of the CEOs who watch him closely. Personally, he is worth about $4 million, invested in short-term Treasury bills to guard himself against conflicts of interest.

His friends and acquaintances say he is a person with a dry wit and patience. Barbara Walters, whom he dated at one time, said of him: "He laughs at himself. I've never heard him sharply cut anyone off. I don't think he has such as a thing as a personal enemy." His current wife once told the *Washington Post*: "One thing that's so refreshing about Alan is that he is up front with people. He doesn't do things behind people's backs."

# Why Has Greenspan Been So Successful?

The simple answer is that monetarism works better than the old theory of supply and demand, but that's not all of it. What makes monetarism so powerful is how Greenspan applies its theory into practice. This speaks as much to his beliefs as his experience, judgment, and personality. Also, even though he dwells in the Washington world of partisan politics, Greenspan has never let political ideology sway his economic decisions. He is a savvy player and a consistent communicator. Call it the Greenspan Way of Monetarism, it has given the United States the longest-lasting growth ever. More people are working, more people own homes, and more companies are profitable than ever in the history of the world. Most important, inflation is under control and stable, which means that consumers, companies, and investors don't have to factor it in when making decisions. This leads to confidence in the economy and a willingness to take risks that lead to further growth and prosperity.

In summary, Alan Greenspan has been successful because he never wavered in his beliefs, which can be summarized as:

### The Lessons of Alan Greenspan

1. Learn everything you can, collect all the data, crunch all the numbers before making a prediction or a financial forecast. Even then, accept and understand that nobody can predict the future when people are involved. Human behavior hasn't changed; people are unpredictable. If you're wrong, correct your mistake and move on.

2. Worry early. Once you see the beginning signs of problems like inflation, it may be too late to prevent it. (This was put best by William McChesney Martin Jr., chairman of the Fed in the 1950s and 1960s, who described the agency this way: Its job is to "take away the punch bowl just as the party gets going.")

3. Inflation or price instability (or uncertainty in any form) is absolutely the worst thing for an economy. It

makes people unwilling to take risks, which are necessary for growth.

4. Take the short-term hit if it will bring long-term gain. Your decisions will not always be popular or politically expedient.

5. Debt is bad. Pay it down as fast as you can.

6. Continue to present your ideas in as many different ways as possible until people understand and act upon what you've been saying. (Greenspan's speeches often begin with mini-lectures about the economy. He hammered away at Congress for years about the issue of debt and deficit reduction until it passed a balanced budget. Now he lectures it on paying down the debt with any surplus that becomes available.)

7. Know the effects of making your decision; understand too, what will happen if you don't make that decision. Consider the worst-case scenario and how you will deal with it.

8. You can never eliminate risk. In fact, you don't want to because it would lead to recklessness. Instead, try to mitigate risk and factor it into your decision-making process.

9. The business cycle is a fact of nature. The best we can do is try to keep the ups and downs from becoming too extreme. Always keep your eyes focused on the big picture despite short-term setbacks or detours.

10. Conditions are always in flux. Be flexible; understand and adjust to the changes around you but remain true to your core convictions.

11. Free, competitive markets, are the most efficient markets. Government intervention should be reserved for crises.

12. In the end, your reputation is your most important asset.

# How to Use This Book

The purpose of this book is to explain how Greenspan has done what he's done and how you can apply some of his economic lessons to your own personal and business life. Because he doesn't give interviews (at least not since becoming Fed chairman), the best picture of what he thinks is seen through his public testimonies, speeches, question-and-answer periods in front of Congress, and the very rare off-the-cuff comment before or after a public appearance. This book is a representation of Greenspan's ideas, in his own words, which are always measured and precise. His thoughts can be crystal clear if you pay close attention. However, he has been accused of obfuscation or being purposely vague. This is a valid criticism, because Greenspan remains sensitive that his remarks can be overanalyzed and misconstrued. By occasionally leaving them open to interpretation, he figures that, on balance, he'll see as many positive reactions as negative ones. As you'll see later, his words do indeed move markets nevertheless.

The quotations that follow have been culled from hundreds of remarks made by Greenspan dating back to the early 1980s. By the way, Greenspan isn't paid for his speeches. The Fed pays for him to fly coach to speaking engagements outside Washington.

Sometimes a short explanation precedes a quotation, because the reader needs to peruse it in historical context to absorb its full impact. Other times, the quotations stand on their own timelessness.

# Greenspan on:
# Banks

**B**ecause of the Fed's role in bank supervision, Greenspan spends a lot of time talking to banking groups. One of his main interests is understanding and refining the line between letting the marketplace determine banks' risk-taking activities and the Fed's job of supervising and reining in these risks. For example, the Fed determines how much money banks must keep in reserve. Keeping too much on hand wastes this resource, but keeping too little on hand won't adequately protect depositors' accounts. In addition, Greenspan appears unsure how far the central bank's safety net should extend in order to keep banks from failing. He believes that failure is a natural part of a free market system and not necessarily bad as long as it doesn't lead to widespread bank failures.

---

"Banks play a crucial role in the financial market infra-structure. When they are undercapitalized, have lax lending standards, and are subjected to weak supervision and regulation, they become a source of systemic risk both domestically and internationally. Despite its importance for distributing savings to their most valued use, short-term interbank funding, especially cross border, may turn out to be the Achilles' heel of an interna-tional financial system that is subject to wide variations in financial confidence. This phenomenon, which is all too

1

common in our domestic experience, may be particularly dangerous in an international setting."

—"Risk Management in the Global Financial System"; at the Annual Financial Markets Conference of the Federal Reserve Bank of Atlanta, Miami Beach, Florida; February 27, 1998

"Improving domestic banking systems in emerging markets will help to limit the toll of the next financial disturbance. But if, as I presume, diversity within the financial sector provides insurance against a financial problem turning into economy-wide distress, then steps to foster the development of capital markets in those economies should also have an especial urgency. Moreover, the difficult groundwork for building the necessary financial infrastructure—improved accounting standards, bankruptcy procedures, legal frameworks, and disclosure—will pay dividends of their own."

—"Do Efficient Financial Markets Mitigate Financial Crises?"; at the 1999 Financial Markets Conference of the Federal Reserve Bank of Atlanta, Sea Island, Georgia; October 19, 1999

• • •

Central banks have oversight of commercial banks, but they can't watch every single transaction. Indeed, they must be careful not to stifle banks.

"The need for a multi-track approach to prudential oversight is particularly evident as we face the reality that the megabanks being formed by growth and consolidation are increasingly complex entities that create the potential for unusually large systemic risks in the national and international economy should they fail. No central bank can fulfill its ultimate responsibilities without endeavoring to ensure that the oversight of such entities is consistent with those potential risks. At the same time, policymakers must be sensitive to the tradeoffs between more detailed supervision and regulation, on the one hand, and moral hazard and the smothering of innovation and competitive response, on the other. Heavier supervision and regulation designed to reduce systemic risk would likely lead to the virtual abdication of risk evaluation by creditors of such entities, who could—in such an environment—rely almost totally on the authorities to discipline and protect the bank. The resultant reduction in market discipline would, in turn, increase the risks in the banking system, quite the opposite of what is intended. Such a heavier hand would also blunt the ability of U.S. banks to respond to crisis events. Increased government regulation is inconsistent with a banking system that can respond to the kinds of changes that have characterized recent years, changes that are expected to accelerate in the years ahead.

—"The Evolution of Bank Supervision"; before the American Bankers Association, Phoenix, Arizona; October 11, 1999

• • •

In September 1997, the international Basle Committee on Banking Supervision, issued 25 principles that represent the basic elements of an effective supervisory system. They were developed among supervisory authorities of the G10 countries and 15 emerging market countries.

"We should always remind ourselves that supervision and regulation are neither infallible nor likely to prove sufficient to meet all our intended goals. Put another way, the Basle standard and the bank examination process, even if both are structured in optimal fashion, are a second line of support for bank soundness. Supervision and regulation can never be a substitute for a bank's own internal scrutiny of its counterparties, as well as the market's scrutiny of the bank. Therefore, we should not, for example, abandon efforts to contain the

scope of the safety net, or to press for increases in the quantity and quality of financial disclosures by regulated institutions."
—AT THE CONFERENCE ON CAPITAL REGULATION IN THE 21ST CENTURY, FEDERAL RESERVE BANK OF NEW YORK, NEW YORK CITY; FEBRUARY 26, 1998

• • •

Central banks can't prevent individual bank failures, but they should prevent bank failures from spreading.

"Our goal as supervisors should not be to prevent all bank failures but to maintain sufficient prudential standards so that banking problems that do occur do not become widespread. We try to achieve the proper balance through official regulations, as well as through formal and informal supervisory policies and procedures."
—"UNDERSTANDING TODAY'S INTERNATIONAL FINANCIAL SYSTEM"; AT THE 34TH ANNUAL CONFERENCE ON BANK STRUCTURE AND COMPETITION OF THE FEDERAL RESERVE BANK OF CHICAGO; MAY 7, 1998

"Providing institutions with the flexibility that may lead to failure is as important as permitting them the opportunity to succeed. By its nature, all business investment is risky. The role of banks to assist in the financing of such risk thus implies the taking of risk by the bank itself. Indeed, this is the economic role of banking in a market economy. The purpose of risk management is not to eliminate risk, but to manage it in a prudent manner."
—AT THE INTERNATIONAL CONFERENCE OF BANKING SUPERVISORS, STOCKHOLM, SWEDEN; JUNE 13, 1996

• • •

The issue of a bank safety net is of great interest to Greenspan. On the one hand, a safety net is necessary to prevent widespread failures. On the other hand, he expresses concern that too great a net allows banks to make unsound investments because they know they will be bailed out.

"The more the safety net is expanded to cover new financial activities the greater the potential that risk-taking will not be subject to market discipline, that bank-like supervision would need to be applied over a wider range, and that financial innovation—the hallmark of the U.S. financial system—will thus be constrained."

—"THE IMPLICATIONS OF TECHNOLOGICAL CHANGES"; BEFORE THE CHARLOTTE CHAMBER OF COMMERCE, CHARLOTTE, NORTH CAROLINA; JULY 10, 1998

"One would like banks to be managed as if there were no safety net—to see their profits reflect solely the value added from intermediation, and not be supplemented, or perhaps even dominated, by the subsidy inherent in the safety net. That is to say, we want to avoid banks' benefiting from risk premiums in their assets that are not reflected fully—if at all—in their liabilities and capital costs.

". . . The safety net has a tendency to benefit speculative and riskier ventures at the expense of sounder ones. Indeed, the safety net tends, other things equal, to increase the nation's overall real rate of interest by facilitating the ability of riskier borrowers to translate their potential credit demands to effective control over resources, crowding out projects that would be economic at lower real rates."

—AT THE FEDERAL RESERVE BANK OF CHICAGO'S ANNUAL CONFERENCE ON BANK STRUCTURE AND COMPETITION; MAY 10, 1990

"Events have made it clear that we ought not to permit banks, because of their access to the safety net, to take excessive risk with inadequate capital. Even if we were to ignore the potential taxpayer costs, we ought not to permit a system that is so inconsistent with efficient market behavior."

—BEFORE THE COMMITTEE ON BANKING, HOUSING, AND URBAN AFFAIRS, U.S. SENATE, JULY 12, 1990

"What is becoming increasingly clear, if it was not before, is that deposit insurance, the Fed Wire, and the liquefication services of central banking are not free lunches. They provide more macro stability, but they misprice risk.

"Our body politic appears to have chosen macro stability. Nonetheless, the costs of the associated safety net have not always been sufficiently considered, and reform in the safety net should be high on our agenda."

—AT THE FEDERAL RESERVE BANK OF CHICAGO'S ANNUAL CONFERENCE ON BANK STRUCTURE AND COMPETITION; MAY 10, 1990

• • •

For the greatest innovation, banks should continue to be regulated on the federal and state level.

"Just as our decentralized banking structure is a key to the robustness of our macroeconomy, a key to the effectiveness of our banking structure is what we term the dual banking system. Our system of both federal and state regulation of banks has fostered a steady stream of innovations that likely would not have proceeded as rapidly or as effectively if our regulatory structure were characterized by a monolithic federal regulator."

—AT THE ANNUAL CONVENTION OF THE INDEPENDENT BANKERS ASSOCIATION OF AMERICA, PHOENIX, ARIZONA; MARCH 22, 1997

"Today, the marketplace for financial services is intensely competitive, innovative, and global. Banks and nonbanks, domestic and foreign, now compete aggressively across a broad range of on- and off-balance-sheet financial activities. It is noteworthy that, for the most part, this transformation has *not* been propelled by sweeping legislative reforms. Rather, the primary driving forces have been advances in computing, telecommunications, and theoretical finance that, taken together, have eroded economic and regulatory barriers to competition, *de facto*. Technology has fundamentally reshaped how financial products are created and how these products are delivered, received, and employed by end-users."

—AT THE CONFERENCE ON BANK STRUCTURE AND COMPETITION OF THE
FEDERAL RESERVE BANK OF CHICAGO, CHICAGO; MAY 1, 1997

"Over the last three decades, the folly of attempting to legislate or regulate against the primal forces of the market is one of the most fundamental lessons learned by banking regulators."

—AT THE CONFERENCE ON BANK STRUCTURE AND COMPETITION OF THE
FEDERAL RESERVE BANK OF CHICAGO, CHICAGO; MAY 1, 1997

• • •

Greenspan is a fan of small, community banks. Despite consolidation and megabanks, he believes these smaller institutions will always have an important role in the banking infrastructure.

"Well-managed, smaller banks have nothing to fear from technology, deregulation, or consolidation. They will continue to play a significant role in the American financial system . . . Many pundits have concluded that these forces will destroy small banks by making them quaint symbols of the past. These prognosticators are plain wrong . . . Meeting customer demands on the customers' terms remains the name of the game and the customer continues to demonstrate his desire to deal with an institution that is conveniently located."

—AT THE INDEPENDENT BANKERS ASSOCIATION OF AMERICA
ANNUAL CONVENTION, NEW ORLEANS; MARCH 18, 1996

"Technology can never fully displace the value of personal contact, the hallmark of community banking."

—"THE IMPLICATIONS OF TECHNOLOGICAL CHANGES";
BEFORE THE CHARLOTTE CHAMBER OF COMMERCE,
CHARLOTTE, NORTH CAROLINA; JULY 10, 1998

• • •

Greenspan could not have envisioned the massive consolidation of banks that occurred in later years.

"I am not in favor of the creation of superbanks. I have always been concerned that bankers too often have looked at where they stand in the list of the *American Banker* with respect to size. I think that attitude really was fairly widespread in the 1960s and the 1970s, (which) is one of the issues which I think has created some of the problems that we have had.

"Size, per se, does not strike me in the normal banking practice of having very much to say for it. All of the evidence that one can see suggests that the economies of scale and scope probably are maximized in relatively small banks, in the areas maybe of $100–$200 million in assets. There is very little evidence that competition between banks above that level gives any specific advantage to the larger institutions.

"Some of our really better banks are not all that large, and I certainly would not argue for any governmental action to create that. Having said that, however, does not mean that I would try, in effect, to inhibit those types of institutions who, in the international arena, believe that increased capital or scope and size are important to them. It's fairly obvious that there are certain types of international transactions which require significant capital. Nonetheless, most types of major loans in the international arena are syndicated in any event, and that can be done by a number of different corporations."

—AT GREENSPAN'S SENATE BANKING COMMITTEE
CONFIRMATION HEARING; JULY 21, 1987

"If a small bank is to be outcompeted, it most likely will be outcompeted by another relatively small bank."

—AT GREENSPAN'S SENATE BANKING COMMITTEE
CONFIRMATION HEARING; JULY 21, 1987

"The optimal failure rate in banking is not zero. Risk-taking means that failures will occur, and, moreover, if we did not permit risk-taking, and therefore the possibility of failure, the banking system would not be in a position to foster economic growth. The banking system would shrink because it would be unable to carry out its underlying economic function."

—AT THE ANNUAL CONVENTION OF THE AMERICAN BANKERS ASSOCIATION, HONOLULU, HAWAII; OCTOBER 5, 1996

• • •

Bankers should not rely solely on arithmetic when granting loans. Personal judgment should play a role.

"The most recent thrust of legislation, and the associated supervision, has virtually eliminated the so-called character loan that had so dominated lending practices of a large number of banks to individuals and small business.

"If regulations require that all loans be based solely on collateral or always documented by full accounting detail, an important part of the credit-granting process that calls for the banker's special expertise will be lost, to the detriment of the economy."

—BEFORE THE TAX FOUNDATION IN NEW YORK; NOVEMBER 18, 1992

• • •

During congressional hearings on reform of the Federal Deposit Insurance Corporation, Greenspan had this to say.

"The subsidy implicit in our current deposit insurance system has stimulated the growth of banks and thrift institutions. In the process, the safety net has distorted market signals to depositors and bankers about the economics of the underlying transactions. This distortion has led depositors to be less cautious in choosing among institutions and has induced some owners and their managers to take excessive risk. In turn, the expanded lending to risky ventures has required increased effort and resources by supervisors and regulators to monitor and modify behavior.

"But in reviewing the list of deficiencies of the deposit insurance system, we should not lose sight of the contribution that both deposit insurance and the discount window have made to macroeconomic stability. The existence and use of the safety net have shielded the broader financial system and the real economy from instabilities in banking markets. More specifically, they have protected the economy from the risk of deposit runs, especially the risk of such runs spreading from bank to bank, disrupting credit and payment flows and the level of trade and commerce. Confidence in the stability of the banking and payments system has been the major reason why the United States has not suffered a financial panic or systemic bank run in the last half century."

—BEFORE THE COMMITTEE ON BANKING, HOUSING,
AND URBAN AFFAIRS, U.S. SENATE; SEPTEMBER 10, 1990

• • •

Always the forecaster, Greenspan views offshore banking as a problem because it interferes with the collection of accurate data.

"The growth of banking in offshore centers suggests that banking is a very mobile industry and that banks and their customers will find perfectly legal ways to avoid the costs of certain kinds of regulations by shifting the booking of their transactions, where such booking shifts need not result in any change in the particular bank with whom they are dealing.

"The migration of banking to offshore centers in response to monetary policy measures is a serious concern. An important issue for the Federal Reserve is that the statistical coverage of banking assets and liabilities of U.S. residents, which is an essential input into the policy process, is compromised as both credits and deposits that formerly were booked in the United States are now recorded offshore. To remedy this problem, we have announced our intention to improve statistics in this area, which should improve our information base for policy-making and the information base available to private market participants."

—*INTERNATIONAL FINANCIAL INTEGRATION;* BEFORE THE FEDERATION OF BANKERS ASSOCIATIONS OF JAPAN, TOKYO; OCTOBER 14, 1992

• • •

Technology can never replace human judgment.

"While new technologies have the potential to unlock efficiencies in financial contracting, they also carry with them risks that need to be understood clearly. For example, understanding the risks, both credit and market risks, of any single off-balance-sheet contract may appear relatively straightforward. However, understanding the aggregate set of risks in a wide assortment of non-standardized contracts is an enormously complex undertaking. Moreover, reliance on advanced technology in the design and monitoring of these contracts cannot be counted on completely to replace informed analytic judgments."

—*INTERNATIONAL FINANCIAL INTEGRATION;* BEFORE THE FEDERATION OF BANKERS ASSOCIATIONS OF JAPAN, TOKYO; OCTOBER 14, 1992

"Credit risk, the risk that a customer will default on an obligation, has been, and remains, the most critical risk to commercial banks and one that must be managed carefully. It may also be the risk in banking that still demands the most subjective judgment, despite constant efforts to improve and quantify the credit decision-making process. Unfortunately, bankers and sometimes their supervisors tend to forget that point and other lessons of the past, as memories fade and conditions change. Bankers pursue faster loan growth, and supervisors hesitate to criticize aggressive practices as long as economic conditions remain favorable. We need to achieve a proper balance to prevent excessive risk-taking, while not discouraging banks from taking risks in responding to legitimate needs of their customers."

—BEFORE THE COMMITTEE ON BANKING, HOUSING, AND URBAN AFFAIRS, U.S. SENATE; SEPTEMBER 22, 1994

• • •

In 1999, President Clinton made history by signing the Gramm-Leach-Bliley Act. This broke down the laws separating commercial and investment banking and prohibiting bank holding companies from underwriting insurance.

Greenspan made sure that everyone knew the Fed's role in the new world of banking.

"The Federal Reserve retains the overall responsibility for financial services holding companies with bank subsidiaries. If the bank is large and/or a significant part of the organization, both law and good supervisory and stabilization policies require an active umbrella supervisor.

"It is clear that the consumer will benefit from the wider permissible scope of activities by, and the more equal competition among, financial entities. . . . Management now will be given greatly enhanced flexibility to determine the best way to deliver its services to the marketplace and the market will judge the correctness of that choice.

". . . There will understandably be some tensions as we all move up the learning curve."

—BEFORE THE AMERICAN COUNCIL OF LIFE INSURANCE'S ANNUAL MEETING, WASHINGTON, D.C.; NOVEMBER 15, 1999

• • •

Taxpayers dislike the idea of paying for bank bailouts, so governments may delay shoring up these failed institutions. This delay can make the situation worse.

"Resolving a banking-sector crisis often involves government outlays because of implicit or explicit government safety net guarantees for banks. Accordingly, the political difficulty in raising taxpayer funds has often encouraged governments to procrastinate and delay resolution, as we saw during our savings and loan crisis. Delay, of course, can add to the fiscal costs and prolong a credit crunch.

"The annals of the United States and others over the past several decades tell us that alternatives within an economy for the process of financial intermediation can protect that economy when one of those financial sectors experiences a shock."

—BEFORE THE WORLD BANK GROUP AND THE INTERNATIONAL MONETARY FUND, PROGRAM OF SEMINARS, WASHINGTON, D.C.; SEPTEMBER 27, 1999

# Greenspan on:
# Capitalism

---

Alan Greenspan is an unabashed capitalist and is not ashamed to sing its praises. He finds the economic system not only more efficient than others but also moral and ethical because it promises the same opportunities to everyone. The system isn't perfect, but it may be the best one around. He's a realist and knows that not everyone succeeds economically in this country, nor are the cards always dealt fairly, but he believes that capitalism, as practiced in the United States, offers the best chance to get ahead for the largest number of people.

This belief in the morality of capitalism may stem from his interest in the works of author Ayn Rand, whose philosophy centers on "rational selfishness." Although capitalism can be thought of as "every man for himself," Rand showed that it can be tempered if everyone understands that it's in his or her own best interest to act properly and fairly. Greenspan, as quoted in a *New York Times* article in 1974, has said that long hours of discussion and argument with Rand made him "think why capitalism is not only efficient and practical but also moral."

---

Economic systems are not only about numbers, facts, and statistics, but also about people. Systems that don't take into account human behavior are doomed to failure.

"History is strewn with examples of economic and social systems that have tried to counter, or alter, human nature and failed. Despite an unrelenting effort over more than seven decades, the system in the Soviet Union was unable to mold human responses to fit the Soviet view of human destiny and how society should be organized. The post mortem of what went wrong clearly exposed the fatal flaws as internal to the system, and not the result of external forces, although the arms race may have hastened the process. The lesson that appears to be emerging is that only free market systems exhibit the flexibility and robustness to accommodate human nature and harness rapidly advancing technology to consistently advance living standards."

—BEFORE THE ANNUAL CONVENTION OF THE AMERICAN SOCIETY OF NEWSPAPER EDITORS, WASHINGTON, D.C.; APRIL 2, 1998

• • •

Greenspan declared capitalism the winner in the contest among economic systems after the fall of the Soviet Union.

"Much of this past century, in effect, has been a test of whether capitalist institutions or more centrally planned socialist institutions would work better, over the long run, in serving the needs of human society.

"Specifically, on November 9, 1989, the Berlin Wall came down, symbolizing the end of an experiment in social policy that began more than four decades earlier with the division of the states of Western and Central Europe into market economies and those governed by state central planning. At the end of World War II, as Winston Churchill put it, 'From Stettin in the Baltic to Trieste in the Adriatic an iron curtain . . . descended across the Continent.' The economies on the Soviet side of the 'curtain' had been, in the prewar period, similar to the market-based economies on the western side. Over four decades both types of economies developed with limited inter-action across the dividing line. It was as close to a controlled experiment in economic systems as could ever be implemented.

"With the books now closed on this experiment, we of course have learned much about how communist economics works, or, more exactly, does not. How highly inefficient prior to 1989 the economies of Eastern Europe and the former Soviet Union were is best illustrated by the fact that energy consumed per unit of output was as much as five to seven times higher than in the West. Moreover, the exceptionally large amount of resources devoted to capital investment, without contributing to the productive capacity of these economies, suggested that these resources were largely wasted.

"In addition, such gaps in efficiency actually understated the gap in performance because they failed to take into account the impact of industrial activity on the environment. The market economies of the West have expanded resources to minimize the adverse impact of industrial activity on the environment. No such resource allocation was made in the Soviet bloc, and the cumulative effect of this neglect is appalling.

"At least for the foreseeable future, the experiment seems to have been concluded overwhelmingly in favor of the free-market capitalist institutions. The bottom line is that coercive societies rarely enhance the state of what we call civilization. But neither do coercive relationships among people."

—"Maintaining Economic Vitality," Millennium Lecture Series, sponsored by the Gerald R. Ford Foundation and Grand Valley State University, Grand Rapids, Michigan; September 8, 1999

"A free-market capitalist system cannot operate fully effectively unless all participants in the economy are given opportunities to achieve their best. If we succeed in opening up opportunities to everyone, our national affluence will almost surely become more widespread. Of even greater import is that all Americans believe that they are part of a system they perceive as fair and worthy of support."

—"Maintaining Economic Vitality," Millennium Lecture Series, sponsored by the Gerald R. Ford Foundation and Grand Valley State University, Grand Rapids, Michigan; September 8, 1999

• • •

Economic systems are rooted in cultural biases and mirror the political system. The lack of political freedom in the Soviet Union and elsewhere is mimicked in an economic system that is tightly controlled, slow moving, and inefficient.

"On the surface, financial infrastructure appears to be a strictly technical concern. It includes accounting standards that accurately portray the condition of the firm, legal systems that reliably provide for the protection of property and the enforcement of contracts, and bankruptcy provisions that lend assurance in advance as to how claims will be resolved in the inevitable result that some business decisions prove to be mistakes. Such an infrastructure in turn promotes transparency within enterprises and corporate governance procedures that will facilitate the trading of claims on businesses in open markets using standardized instruments rather than idiosyncratic bank loans. But the development of such institutions is almost invariably molded by the culture of a society. The antipathy to the "loss of face" in Asia makes it difficult to institute, for example, the bankruptcy procedures of western nations. And even the latter differ from one another owing to deep-seated differences in views of creditor-debtor relationships. Arguably the notion of property rights in today's Russia is subliminally biased by a Soviet education that inculcated a highly negative view of individual property ownership."

—before the World Bank Group and the International Monetary Fund, Program of Seminars, Washington, D.C.; September 27, 1999

• • •

Always the economist, Greenspan puts a dollar value on discrimination.

"Discrimination is patently immoral, but it is now increasingly being seen as unprofitable. Prices, interest rates, stock prices, and other signals produced by market economies to encourage the distribution of productive resources have no inherent moral content. However, to the extent that market participants discriminate—consciously or, more likely, unconsciously—the setting of wages and prices and the distribution of output are distorted. In the end, costs are higher, less real output is produced, and national wealth accumulation is slowed. If markets were fully efficient—that is, if all resources were allocated optimally and fully employed without discrimination—profit maximizes would arbitrage away such non-economic differences in the returns to human capital and other productive resources."

—*THE UNDEREMPLOYMENT OF MINORITIES;* AT THE WALL STREET PROJECT
ANNIVERSARY CONFERENCE OF THE RAINBOW/PUSH COALITION,
NEW YORK; JANUARY 16, 1998

• • •

Greenspan makes mention of "creative destruction" in many presentations. He considers it a hallmark of free economies, keeping them fresh and innovative.

"Market economies are driven by what Professor Joseph Schumpeter, a number of decades ago, called 'creative destruction.' By this he meant newer ways of doing things, newer products, and novel engineering and architectural insights that induce the continuous obsolescence and retirement of factories and equipment and a reshuffling of workers to new and different activities. Market economies in that sense are continuously renewing themselves. Innovation, risk-taking, and competition are the driving forces that propel standards of living progressively higher."

—BEFORE THE ANNUAL CONVENTION OF THE AMERICAN SOCIETY OF NEWSPAPER EDITORS, WASHINGTON, D.C.; APRIL 2, 1998

"My sense is that one consequence of this Asian crisis is an increasing awareness in the region that market capitalism, as practiced in the West, especially in the United States, is the superior model; that is, it provides greater promise of producing rising standards of living and continuous growth."

—THE CURRENT ASIAN CRISIS AND THE FINANCIAL RESOURCES OF THE IMF; BEFORE THE COMMITTEE ON AGRICULTURE, U.S. HOUSE OF REPRESENTATIVES; MAY 21, 1998

• • •

Although not always perfect, capitalism provides checks and balances against destructive monopolies.

"Through skill, perseverance, luck, or political connections, competitors have always pressed for market dominance. It is free, open markets that act to thwart achievement of such dominance, and in the process direct the competitive drive, which seeks economic survival, toward the improvement of products, greater productivity, and the amassing and distribution of wealth."

—"THE EFFECTS OF MERGERS"; BEFORE THE COMMITTEE ON THE JUDICIARY, U.S. SENATE; JUNE 16, 1998

"In one sense, markets generally are always in some state of imperfection in that businesses never fully exploit, perhaps can never fully exploit, all opportunities for profitable, productive, investment. Consumers do not always seek out the lowest prices or the best quality, owing to the costs of searching across sellers. Rationally acting individuals may choose not to exert the additional effort that they perceive will only marginally enhance their state of well-being. Then, of course, people do not always act rationally."

> —*"The Effects of Mergers";* before the Committee on the Judiciary, U.S. Senate; June 16, 1998

• • •

Greenspan would prefer that free markets control themselves but knows that government must step in to keep the players honest.

"Any voluntary transaction comprises not only a good or a service but a representation, explicit or otherwise, of the nature of the product being transferred. Misrepresentation to induce an exchange is theft, in that the transaction was not voluntary. Laws against fraud are demonstrably a necessary fixture of any free market economy."

> —*"The Effects of Mergers";* before the Committee on the Judiciary, U.S. Senate; June 16, 1998

• • •

Capitalist systems are always renewing themselves, moving toward a state of ever-higher efficiency.

"The American economy, like all advanced capitalist economies, is continually in the process of what Joseph Schumpeter, a number of decades ago, called 'creative destruction.' Capital equipment, production processes, financial and labor market infrastructure, and the whole panoply of private institutions that make up a market economy are always in a state of flux—in almost all cases evolving into more efficient regimes."

> —"Question: Is There a New Economy?"; at the Haas Annual Business Faculty Research Dialogue, University of California, Berkeley, California; September 4, 1998

"Much of what we took for granted in our free market system and assumed to be human nature was not nature at all, but culture. The dismantling of the central planning function in an economy does not, as some had supposed, automatically establish a free market entrepreneurial system. There is a vast amount of capitalist culture and infrastructure underpinning market economies that has evolved over generations: laws, conventions, behaviors, and a wide variety of business professions and practices that have no important functions in a centrally planned economy."

—AT THE WOODROW WILSON AWARD DINNER OF THE WOODROW WILSON INTERNATIONAL CENTER FOR SCHOLARS, NEW YORK CITY; JUNE 10, 1997

• • •

One reason for the failure of the Soviet system was a lack of accurate data on the economy. Without it, planners could not see changes that were coming and react appropriately.

"One might think that the planning authorities (Soviet Union) should have been able to adjust to these distortions. They tried. But they faced insurmountable handicaps in that they did not have access to the immediate signals of price changes that so efficiently clear markets in capitalist economies. Just as important, they did not have the signals of finance to adjust the allocation of physical resources to accommodate the shifting tastes of consumers."

—AT THE WOODROW WILSON AWARD DINNER OF THE WOODROW WILSON INTERNATIONAL CENTER FOR SCHOLARS, NEW YORK CITY; JUNE 10, 1997

• • •

Greenspan believes in transparency, the dissemination of the most amount of information in the most timely manner. This is not only fair, but makes markets more efficient in the long run.

"For a market economy to function effectively, there must also be widespread dissemination of timely financial and other relevant information. This enables market participants to make the type of informed judgments that foster the most efficient allocation of capital—efficient in the sense that our physical resources are directed at producing those goods and services most valued by consumers. This requires a free press and government data information systems that are perceived to be free of hidden political manipulation."

—AT THE WOODROW WILSON AWARD DINNER OF THE WOODROW WILSON INTERNATIONAL CENTER FOR SCHOLARS, NEW YORK CITY; JUNE 10, 1997

• • •

The world's economies are moving toward capitalism. Greenspan views it almost as part of the world's natural order.

"Despite the ebb and flow of governments of differing persuasions, the face of the world economy continues to edge toward free-market-oriented societies. This is especially the case as increasing numbers of transition economies prosper and emerging market economies wedded to free-market paradigms grow impressively.

"There has been, to be sure, much pain and periodic backtracking among a number of the nations that discarded the mantle of central planning. There will doubtless be more. But the experience of the last half century clearly attests to how far the power of the idea of market freedom can carry."

—AT THE WOODROW WILSON AWARD DINNER OF THE WOODROW WILSON INTERNATIONAL CENTER FOR SCHOLARS, NEW YORK CITY; JUNE 10, 1997

"The good performance of the American economy in the most fundamental sense rests on the actions of millions of people, who have been given the scope to express themselves in free and open markets. In this, we are a model for the rest of

the world, which has come to appreciate the power of market economies to provide for the public's long-term welfare."
—BEFORE THE COMMITTEE ON BANKING, HOUSING, AND URBAN AFFAIRS, U.S. SENATE; JULY 18, 1996

"What we do know is that, excluding the sorrowful period of the Dark Ages, human knowledge has rarely been lost, nor technology reversed, and so one can presume that we will evolve in the twenty-first century and beyond in ways not now foreseeable. We can anticipate change to be pervasive and, if competitive forces are allowed free rein, and our fiscal problems resolved, we can expect ever higher living standards for all Americans."
—BEFORE THE ECONOMIC CLUB OF CHICAGO, CHICAGO; OCTOBER 19, 1995

• • •

In most cases, the marketplace knows best. A group of economists cannot do better.

Q. Do we need more government planning by some agency such as the Council of Economic Advisors?
A. That question presupposes that economists have quite considerable insight into economic processes and great capacity to fine-tune them—for example, that we can foresee shortages and head them off if we have adequate manpower or womanpower or computer-power. This is highly questionable.
We do have quite good tools, and we can make some very useful and valuable judgments. But it is very difficult to improve on the allocation processes of the marketplace.
—"WHY BUSINESS WILL CONTINUE ON THE UPSWING"; INTERVIEW WITH ALAN GREENSPAN, CHAIRMAN, COUNCIL OF ECONOMIC ADVISORS; *U.S. NEWS & WORLD REPORT,* JUNE 28, 1976

# Greenspan on:

# Competition

A s a free-market proponent, Greenspan is a fan of robust competition both domestically and internationally. Indeed, competition must exist for an economy to grow and prosper.

"In the end it is clear that all economic progress rests on competition."
—BEFORE THE DALLAS AMBASSADORS FORUM, DALLAS, TEXAS; APRIL 16, 1999

• • •

Here, Greenspan is referring to his forecasting company, Townsend-Greenspan & Co.

"When I was in the private sector, I hated competition, but I recognized that it made me work better."
—BEFORE THE COMMITTEE ON BANKING, HOUSING, AND URBAN AFFAIRS, U.S. SENATE; FEBRUARY 20, 1996

• • •

Older technologies must compete with new technologies for a place in the economy.

"As we contemplate the appropriate public policies for an economy experiencing rapid technology advancement, we should strive to maintain the flexibility of our labor and capital markets that has spurred the continuous replacement of capital facilities embodying older technologies with facilities reflecting the newest innovations. Further reducing regulatory impediments to competition, will, of course, add to this process. The newer technologies have widened the potential for economic well-being. Governments should seek to foster that potential."

—"HIGH-TECH INDUSTRY IN THE U.S. ECONOMY"; BEFORE THE JOINT ECONOMIC COMMITTEE, U.S. CONGRESS; JUNE 14, 1999

• • •

Sometimes, competition isn't pretty. Greenspan notes that if policymakers protect companies (or countries) from competitors, they stifle the best part of capitalism, the urge to innovate and strive for better products and services.

"For good or ill, an unforgiving capitalist process is driving wealth creation. It has become increasingly difficult for policymakers who wish to practice, as they put it, a more 'caring' capitalism to realize the full potential of their economies. Their choices have become limited. To the extent they block themselves or portions of their population from what they perceive as harsh competitive pressures, they must accept a lower average standard of living for their populace. As a consequence, increasingly, nations appear to be opting to open themselves to competition, however harsh, and become producers that can compete in world markets. Not irrelevant to the choice is that major advances in telecommunications have made it troublesome for politicians and policymakers to go too far in preempting market forces when the material affluence of market-based economies has become so evident to ubiquitous television watchers, their constituents, around the world."

—BEFORE THE ANNUAL CONVENTION OF THE AMERICAN SOCIETY OF
NEWSPAPER EDITORS, WASHINGTON, D.C.; APRIL 2, 1998

• • •

Just because a company is big doesn't mean it should be targeted by antitrust busters. On the other hand, the market-place—in the form of shareholder pressure—should force large companies to change their size if it's getting in the way of their efficiency.

"Unless a relationship between bigness and market concentration can be more firmly rooted in anti-competitive behavior, bigness, per se, does not appear to be an issue for national economic policy. Rather, it appears that bigness should be primarily the concern of shareholders whose returns could be muted by large company inefficiencies, and their customers who may face bureaucratic inflexibility."

—"THE EFFECTS OF MERGERS"; BEFORE THE COMMITTEE ON THE JUDICIARY,
U.S. SENATE; JUNE 16, 1998

• • •

Large companies don't last long just because they're large. They must also be efficient.

"I am not saying that dominant positions in industries cannot be maintained for extended periods, but I suspect in free competitive markets that it is possible only if dominance is maintained through cost efficiencies and low prices that competitors have difficulty matching. By the measure of what benefits consumers, such enterprises should not be discouraged."

—"THE EFFECTS OF MERGERS"; BEFORE THE COMMITTEE ON THE JUDICIARY,
U.S. SENATE; JUNE 16, 1998

"If competitors are excluded because of a company's excellence in addressing consumer needs, should such activity be constrained by law? Such a standard, if generally applied to business initiatives, would have chilled the type of competitive aggressiveness that brings efficiencies and innovation to the marketplace."
—"THE EFFECTS OF MERGERS"; BEFORE THE COMMITTEE ON THE JUDICIARY, U.S. SENATE; JUNE 16, 1998

"We do not have and cannot have the resources required to fully understand the implications of mergers. Forecasting how markets or technologies will evolve is an excruciatingly difficult task. We sometimes do it reasonably well and sometimes we do it poorly."
—"THE EFFECTS OF MERGERS"; BEFORE THE COMMITTEE ON THE JUDICIARY, U.S. SENATE; JUNE 16, 1998

• • •

If economies are to grow and prosper, competition must be encouraged. One of the reasons why centrally planned economies like those found in Eastern Bloc nations failed was because competition was stifled.

"In any event, realizing the full potential of these powerful new technologies is going to depend on the prevalence of another fundamental of economic growth—competition. We seem to have learned in recent years that growth can be hobbled by unnecessary or poorly designed regulation and by protection of business through barriers to free trade within a country and with other countries. Indeed, the unquestioned lesson of the failures of economic development in Eastern Europe after World War II is that government central planning was incompatible with a vibrant economy. It suppressed the forces of competition and, almost surely as a consequence, stifled economic progress and growth as well.

Virtually all of those countries are now endeavoring to build free-market, competitive economies as rapidly as possible.

"The incentives associated with a competitive market are critical in determining the degree to which our endowments of natural resources and human skills are turned into wealth. If market forces are inhibited, wealth creation is almost certain to be disappointing. It is almost surely the case that the development of the computer industry has done more to enhance the efficiency of American business generally than any other recent phenomenon. While the early development of mainframe computers was heavily concentrated in large corporate enterprises, the industry as we know it today owes much to the subsequent birth and growth of many smaller and more dynamic firms."

—BEFORE THE ECONOMIC CLUB OF CHICAGO, CHICAGO; OCTOBER 19, 1995

# Greenspan on:

# Debt and Deficits

From his earliest days, even before he was Fed chairman, Greenspan railed against the national debt. His argument was simple: Debt robs the system of money that could be used for economic expansion. Another source of funding for economic growth could be from private savings, but that level is too low, Greenspan concludes.

The Fed has virtually no control over the country's debt. That's a spending/taxing function of Congress, which finally saw a balanced budget plan under President Clinton. What to do with any surplus from the balanced budget? Greenspan calls for a systematic retirement of the debt. Only in this way can the economic expansion continue.

In his quest to persuade Congress over the years to pay down the debt, Greenspan uses every argument imaginable to show how the national debt causes a multitude of economic woes. He has been relentless on the issue.

"The deficit is a malignant force in our economy. How the deficit is reduced is very important; that it be done is crucial. Allowing it to fester would court a dangerous erosion of our economic strength and a potentially significant deterioration in our real standard of living. Fortunately, we have it in our power to reverse this process. This committee has an important role in this process. Speaking as a citizen, I wish you well."

—BEFORE THE COMMITTEE ON FINANCE,
U.S. SENATE; MARCH 24, 1993

"There is nothing special about the budget balance per se, except that it is far superior to deficits. I have always emphasized the value of a budgetary surplus in increasing national savings, especially when American private domestic savings is low, as it is today. Higher national savings lead in the long run to higher investment and living standards. They also foster low inflation. Low inflation itself may be responsible, in part, for higher productivity growth and larger gains in standards of living."

—BEFORE THE COMMITTEE ON THE BUDGET, U.S. HOUSE OF
REPRESENTATIVES; OCTOBER 8, 1997

"The deficit dropped to its lowest level in more than two decades in fiscal 1997, and yesterday the Congressional Budget Office released projections that show the budget remaining essentially in balance over the next few years, moving to annual surpluses equal to 1 percent of GDP by the middle of the next decade. The reduction in federal borrowing to date and in prospect is already paying off for the U.S. economy by helping hold down long-term interest rates and, in turn, providing support to private capital spending and other interest-sensitive outlays."

—"THE CURRENT FISCAL SITUATION"; BEFORE THE COMMITTEE ON THE
BUDGET, U.S. SENATE; JANUARY 29, 1998

• • •

Greenspan's preference is to use any surplus money to pay down the national debt. That would help pull down interest rates and better prepare the nation for the expected surge of baby-boom retirements.

"Things are happening which we call technical factors, which is another way of saying we don't have a clue, and they could just as readily go in the other direction. If you start to simulate a number of these things that could go wrong, those surpluses evaporate fairly rapidly—at least the size of them shrinks dramatically."

—BEFORE THE SENATE BANKING COMMITTEE; JULY 28, 1999

"I have always emphasized that we should be aiming for budgetary surpluses and using the proceeds to retire outstanding federal debt. This would put further downward pressure on long-term interest rates, which would enhance private capital investment, labor productivity, and economic growth. The out-pouring of proposals for using the anticipated surplus does not bode well for the prospect of maintaining fiscal discipline."

—"THE CURRENT FISCAL SITUATION"; BEFORE THE COMMITTEE ON THE BUDGET, U.S. SENATE; JANUARY 29, 1998

•  •  •

Although he wasn't referring specifically to Japan's reluctance to deal with nonperforming loans, Greenspan makes the point that it's always best to pay off these loans and move on.

"It is becoming increasingly evident that nonperforming loans should be dealt with expeditiously. The expected values of the losses on these loans are, of course, a subtraction from capital. But since these estimates are uncertain, they embody an additional risk premium that reduces the markets' best estimate of the size of effective equity capital even if capital is replenished. It is, hence, far better to remove these dubious assets and their associated risk premium from bank balance sheets, and dispose of them separately, preferably promptly."

—"RISK MANAGEMENT IN THE GLOBAL FINANCIAL SYSTEM"; BEFORE THE ANNUAL FINANCIAL MARKETS CONFERENCE OF THE FEDERAL RESERVE BANK OF ATLANTA, MIAMI BEACH, FLORIDA; FEBRUARY 27, 1998

• • •

During his mid-year economic review and testimony to Congress in 1998, Greenspan said the economy was as impressive as he had seen it in 50 years. Lawmakers asked him what could be done to continue this run.

"The one thing that can go wrong in this whole process is that we think we've got a whole big bundle of cash, we commit it to the future, and we find that most of it isn't there.

". . . As I have emphasized many times, lower budget deficits are the surest and most direct way to increase national saving. Higher national saving would help to reduce real interest rates further, promoting more rapid accumulation of productive capital embodying recent technological advances. Agreement is widely shared that attaining a higher national saving rate quite soon is crucial, particularly in view of the anticipated shift in the nation's demographics in the first few decades of the next century."
—BEFORE THE HOUSE COMMITTEE ON THE BUDGET; MARCH 27, 1996

"Alexander Hamilton recognized, and we should never forget, that investors have many choices on world markets. Even the whiff of the possibility that the United States would not honor its debt would push up the cost of borrowing for years to come. Alexander Hamilton drew a line that no one should cross: the government of the United States must never default on its debt."
—BEFORE THE PUBLIC SECURITIES ASSOCIATION, NEW YORK; OCTOBER 7, 1996

• • •

Domestic savings levels must be increased to sustain our growing economy. An alternative is to retire the debt.

"The challenge for the United States over the coming decades is clear. We must sustain higher levels of investment if we are to achieve healthy increases in productivity and be strong and successful competitors in the international marketplace. To support that investment, we shall need to raise the level of domestic saving. Absent a rise in private saving, it will be necessary to eliminate the structural deficit in the federal budget. Indeed, it has long been my judgment that it would be wise to target achievement of at least a modest surplus down the road."

—BEFORE THE COMMITTEE ON THE BUDGET, U.S. SENATE; JANUARY 26, 1995

SEN. JIM BUNNING (R–Kentucky): How do you propose we increase domestic savings then?

GREENSPAN: We have gone through innumerable measures to increase private savings, and at best we have to argue that the results were mixed because we do not see any profound increase in private savings in this county. One of the reasons I have argued for allowing the surpluses to run is it creates a savings for private investment. If we can't do it in the private accounts, a second best condition is to allow surpluses to emerge, and finance the necessary investment to create the continued acceleration in productivity as a result of these investments that we've seen over the last five to eight years. Nonetheless, Senator, I do think it is important for us to focus on means of achieving higher levels of private savings.

—BEFORE THE SENATE BANKING COMMITTEE; JANUARY 26, 2000

"There is no doubt, in my judgment, that the net result of moving to budget balance will be a more efficient, more productive U.S. economy."

—"HUMPHREY-HAWKINS, MONETARY POLICY TESTIMONY AND REPORT TO THE CONGRESS"; JULY 19, 1995

Q: Let me ask about the political implication of what happened this past week. You're not only an economist; you're a pretty seasoned watcher of Washington at work. What the president seems to have done in the view of many of the people in the Senate is to undercut that Senate initiative and strike a separate deal with the House Democrats. Where does this leave the politics of deficit control as we look out toward the next budget and the years beyond?

A: It clearly undercuts any serious attempt to come to grips with the long-term expenditure problems. The difficulty is that the House—and, I fear, in part the president—is trying in some way or another to be responsive to constituents' views on this budget. The problem, unfortunately, is that the polls very obviously tell us that the public is for a lower deficit, no tax increase, and only negligible cuts in outlays, which is another way of saying they are also implicitly for the repeal of the laws of arithmetic.

—"An Interview with Alan Greenspan, Council of Economic Advisers"; *The Washington Post,* August 4, 1985

Q. Do federal deficits really matter, then?

A. They do indeed. Deficits are important—largely because when the federal government borrows, it pre-empts moneys needed by others since it is willing to pay any interest rate. Thus, it crowds private borrowers out of the capital markets. They then tend to go to their commercial banks for funding. Commercial bankers generally will seek out shorter-term funds to meet the requirements of their customers, which leads to higher interest rates throughout the economy.

Ultimately, very large continuing deficits create a major expansion in the money supply, which will inevitably drive up the rate of inflation as well. And it's that process that the financial community around the world perceives as pending. That's the reason nominal long-term interest rates are so high and why they threaten the expansion of all types of assets that require long-term financing.

Q. Does it make any difference whether deficits are cut through taxation, spending cuts or a combination?

A. My personal preference would be to lean completely on spending. But that is probably not possible. However, increases in taxes, unrelated to any other action on the budget, are more likely to act to finance higher expenditures than to cut the deficit. That's a Capitol Hill psychology; it's not an economic law. So my expectation is that this issue, if it is to be dealt with in a politically realistic way, will have a combination of expenditure restraint tied to tax increases.

—"THE LONG-TERM BOOM NOW IN PROSPECT," INTERVIEW WITH ALAN GREENSPAN, LEADING ECONOMIST AND UNOFFICIAL ADVISOR TO PRESIDENT FORD; *U.S. NEWS & WORLD REPORT,* JUNE 6, 1983

Q. Mr. Greenspan, the federal government's debt is about to hit a trillion dollars. How much of a cause for concern is that to you?

A. The trillion-dollar figure is, in and of itself, not important. It is important because it is symbolic—as a clue to the fact that we have accumulated an awful lot of nonproductive federal borrowing. Government debt, by its very nature, can not be used for productive purposes.

The absolute size of that debt is not critical. What is is the change from year to year in the proportion of new savings that are taken up by federal borrowing. That has been increasing steadily and is, in my judgment, the major force which is propelling the inflation in this country.

Q. Isn't the rise in private debt dangerous, too?

A. Not like federal debt. Economists tend to view whether debt is inflationary or not inflationary, or bad or good, only in terms of what it's used for. In that sense, there is no limit to the size of private debt, provided it is used for productive purposes.

—"ARE AMERICANS GOING TOO DEEP INTO DEBT?",
INTERVIEW WITH ALAN GREENSPAN, ECONOMIST;
*U.S. NEWS & WORLD REPORT,* AUGUST 3, 1981

• • •

Through a chain of events, the debt also affects the value of the U.S. dollar.

"It is important to understand just how this link between lower domestic savings and increased inflows from abroad worked in practice. The increased demand for funds to finance both the gaping budget deficit and growing private investment in the face of a declining private savings rate put substantial upward pressure on U.S. interest rates. Higher interest rates made investment in the United States more attractive to foreigners, increased demand for dollars to implement such investments, and, thereby, pushed up the foreign exchange value of the dollar. The higher dollar, in turn, reduced U.S. international price competitiveness and contributed to the widening of the external deficit. The fiscal stimulus and downtrend in private savings also led to strong growth in U.S. domestic demand, which raised demand for imports and contributed further to the external deficit."

—BEFORE THE COMMITTEE ON WAYS AND MEANS,
U.S. HOUSE OF REPRESENTATIVES; JANUARY 25, 1990

"The persistence of inadequate domestic savings, large current account deficits, and continued deterioration of the U.S. net international investment position remain matters of serious concern. Current U.S. savings levels are inadequate to finance the domestic investment necessary to provide rising living standards for future generations on the scale enjoyed by previous generations. The most important contribution the Congress can make to remedying this problem is to continue the progress made in recent years in reducing the federal budget deficit. As I have stated here before, the ultimate target should be a budget surplus."

—BEFORE THE COMMITTEE ON WAYS AND MEANS,
U.S. HOUSE OF REPRESENTATIVES; JANUARY 25, 1990

"Deficits are damaging because they pull resources away from private investment, reducing the rate of growth of the nation's capital stock. This, in turn, means less capital per worker than would otherwise be the case and engenders, over the long run, a slower growth in labor productivity and, with it, a slower growth in our standard of living."

—BEFORE THE BIPARTISAN COMMISSION ON ENTITLEMENT AND
TAX REFORM, WASHINGTON, D.C.; JULY 15, 1994

"Time is no longer on our side. Any presumption that the deficit is benign is clearly false. This is especially the case with so low a private saving rate. Under current law, the deficit will begin to climb again by the end of the decade. Moreover, demographic trends imply an inexorable upward path for government expenditures as the next century unfolds. Allowing this to happen courts a marked sapping of our economy's vitality. The longer we wait, the more draconian the remedies will have to be. We must particularly eschew moving our programs off-budget. This is mere bookkeeping. There is no way around the need to deal with the allocation of real resources, and we must address that fact head-on."

—BEFORE THE BIPARTISAN COMMISSION ON ENTITLEMENT AND
TAX REFORM, WASHINGTON, D.C.; JULY 15, 1994

• • •

The budget deficit should not be paid down by increasing taxes.

"All else equal, reducing the deficit would enlarge the pool of savings available for private capital investment. But investment will not automatically occur unless there are adequate incentives for risk-taking. A greater willingness of a society to consume less of its current income should lower real interest rates and spur such investment. But if risk-taking is discouraged through excessive taxation of capital or repressive regulation, high levels of investment will not emerge and the level of saving will fall as real incomes stagnate."

—BEFORE THE COMMITTEE ON FINANCE, U.S. SENATE; MARCH 24, 1993

• • •

Hoping to sell Congress on paying down the debt while maintaining popular social program spending, Greenspan suggests that some of these programs have set time limits.

"While there is no substitute for political will in reining in outsized structural budget deficits, there are changes, I believe, that could make the budget process more effective. In particular, it is worth reconsidering sunset legislation, which would impose explicit termination dates on spending programs. Expiring programs that still have merit should have no difficulty being reauthorized, but programs whose justification has become less compelling would not receive the necessary votes. Indeed, it is hard to imagine that sunset legislation would not lead to at least some improvement over the current situation, quite possibly fostering nontrivial budget savings."

—BEFORE THE COMMITTEE ON FINANCE, U.S. SENATE; MARCH 24, 1993

# Greenspan on:
# Derivatives

---

Alan Greenspan and the Federal Reserve locked their radar screens on derivatives in the early 1980s, taking notice when some investors complained about losing large amounts of money on derivatives schemes that seemed shaky. Derivatives are often combinations of puts, calls, swaps, futures, options, and so on, all having a time value or time constriction placed on the deal. They often involve commodities such as precious metals, currencies, and agricultural products. Sometimes they simply involve a financial instrument such as an S & P future. The key element to all of these deals is that they involve betting against a future price—either up or down. In addition, they tend to be sensitive to interest rates, which is where they crossed paths with the Fed.

---

Greenspan sees nothing intrinsically wrong with derivatives, but does acknowledge dangerous aspects of their use especially to those who may not be sophisticated enough to understand their intricacies.

"While derivatives have enhanced the overall efficiency of financial markets and the economy, the Board recognizes that some derivatives are complex instruments that, if not properly understood and managed, can pose risks to individual users and possibly also to the overall stability of the financial system.

"The risks to individual institutions have been underscored by press reports of losses on certain derivatives contracts in the wake of the recent sharp increases in interest rates here and abroad.

"Case studies of these episodes undoubtedly will offer useful insights to users of derivatives and to policymakers. But it would be wrong to draw sweeping conclusions from these events."

—BEFORE THE HOUSE SUBCOMMITTEE ON TELECOMMUNICATIONS
AND FINANCE; MAY 25, 1994

• • •

Greenspan calls on market forces to keep traders honest, saying that regulators have a hard time discovering questionable manipulation. Here, he refers to the Hunt brothers' ill-fated attempt to corner the silver market, which left markets shaky in its wake.

"Securities regulators have difficulty ferreting out malfeasance. Even trading on exchanges does not in itself eliminate all endeavors at manipulation, as the Hunt brothers' 1979–80 fiasco in silver demonstrated. The primary source of regulatory effectiveness has always been private traders being knowledgeable of their counterparties. Government regulation can only act as a backup. It should be careful not to create net benefits to markets."

—"THE REGULATION OF OTC DERIVATIVES"; BEFORE THE COMMITTEE ON
BANKING AND FINANCIAL SERVICES, U.S. HOUSE OF REPRESENTATIVES;
JULY 24, 1998

"Dealers are established institutions with substantial assets and significant investments in their reputations. When they have been seen to engage in deceptive practices, the professional counterparties that have been victimized have been able to obtain redress under laws applicable to contracts generally. Moreover, the threat of legal damage awards provides dealers with strong incentives to avoid misconduct.

"A far more powerful incentive, however, is the fear of loss of the dealer's good reputation, without which it cannot compete effectively, regardless of its financial strength or financial engineering capabilities."

—"THE REGULATION OF OTC DERIVATIVES";
BEFORE THE COMMITTEE ON BANKING AND FINANCIAL
SERVICES, U.S. HOUSE OF REPRESENTATIVES; JULY 24, 1998

• • •

Greenspan believes that if government regulators were to step in and try to prevent or mitigate losses in the derivatives markets, investors might engage in even more risky behavior, which could lead to unstable markets. He says that regulators' role is to make sure that each side understands its responsibilities and subsequent consequences of its action.

"Markets function most efficiently when both parties to financial transactions are free to enter into transactions at their own discretion, unhampered by any perceived need to serve the interests of their counterparties. To date, losses in the financial markets have not led to broader systemic problems. Moreover, both dealers and their customers, somewhat shaken by the volatility of recent markets, are responding to these events by exercising greater caution. If discipline from incurring losses from mistakes were mitigated, vigilance would be relaxed, the market's natural adaptive response would be blunted, and the value of decentralized market decisions as allocators of scarce capital resources would be reduced. I believe that we should start with the principle that parties to financial transactions are responsible for their own decisions and only use regulation to adjust the balance of responsibilities between the parties cautiously after the benefit has been clearly established."

—BEFORE THE COMMITTEE ON BANKING, HOUSING, AND URBAN AFFAIRS, U.S. SENATE; JANUARY 5, 1995

• • •

Shady financial operators sometimes work offshore to try to hide their handiwork away from government regulators. Greenspan calls on regulators worldwide to make sure that they work in concert to stem the shockwaves from derivatives activities.

"Even if derivatives activities are not themselves a source of systemic risk, they may help speed the transmission of a shock from some other source to other markets and institutions. Linkages among financial markets, both domestically and internationally, have become considerably tighter in recent years. Derivatives have contributed to this development, although other forces—the increasing importance of institutional investors, improvements in information and telecommunications technology, and the removal of capital controls by many countries—clearly have been at work. Given these tighter linkages, if a major international financial firm came under severe financial stress, authorities could face significant difficulties in containing the effects on other institutions and markets. At a minimum, success would require close coordination with relevant authorities in the home country and abroad."

—BEFORE THE HOUSE SUBCOMMITTEE ON TELECOMMUNICATIONS AND FINANCE; MAY 25, 1994

"There is little doubt that under the gold standard the restraint on both public and private credit creation limited price inflation, but it was also increasingly perceived as too restrictive to government discretion. The abandonment of the domestic convertibility of gold effectively augmented the power of the monetary authorities to create claims. Possibly as a consequence, post–World War II fluctuations in gross domestic product have been somewhat less than those prior to the 1930s, and no major economic contraction of the dimensions experienced in earlier years has occurred in major industrial countries. On the other hand, peace-time inflation has been far more virulent."

—AT THE CATHOLIC UNIVERSITY LEUVEN, LEUVEN, BELGIUM;
JANUARY 14, 1997

• • •

In 1998, Greenspan took some his sharpest criticism ever from those who said the Fed had no business interfering in the bailout of Long Term Capital Management, a Greenwich, Connecticut–based hedge fund that suffered about $4 billion in losses because of high-risk, high-leverage stock and bond trades. Equally vexing to his supporters was that it seemed as though Greenspan had gone against his free market beliefs and inserted the Fed into the situation instead of letting the market take care of it.

The Federal Reserve Bank of New York helped organize a takeover of LTCM by 14 banks and brokerage firms, which included Merrill Lynch, Chase Manhattan, Bankers Trust, Morgan Stanley Dean Witter, J. P. Morgan, Goldman Sachs, Salomon Smith Barney, and several European banks.

LTCM's wealthy investors took a bath when the company's computer models—which showed a profit no matter which way the market went—didn't account for the collapse of the Russian ruble in late August and the international financial crisis that followed. Greenspan justified the Fed's action by saying it prevented a possible global collapse.

"The Federal Reserve Bank of New York's efforts were designed solely to enhance the probability of an orderly private-sector adjustment, not to dictate the path that adjustment would take. No Federal Reserve funds were put at risk, no promises were made by the Federal Reserve, and no individual firms were pressured to participate.

"Officials of the Federal Reserve Bank of New York facilitated discussions in which the private parties arrived at an agreement that both served their mutual self-interest and avoided possible serious market dislocations.

". . . In our dynamic market economy, investors and traders, at times, make misjudgments. Any time that there is public involvement that softens the blow of private-sector losses—even as obliquely as in this episode—the issue of moral hazard arises. Any action by the government that prevents some of the negative consequences to the private sector of the mistakes it makes raises the threshold of risks market participants will presumably subsequently choose to take. Over time, economic efficiency will be impaired as some uneconomic investments are undertaken under the implicit assumption that possible losses may be borne by the government.

". . . The Federal Reserve provided its good offices to LTCM's creditors, not to protect LTCM's investors, creditors, or managers from loss, but to avoid the distortions to market processes caused by a fire-sale liquidation and the consequent spreading of those distortions through contagion. To be sure, this may well work to reduce the ultimate losses to the original owners of LTCM, but that was a byproduct, perhaps unfortunate, of the process.

"Had the failure of LTCM triggered the seizing up of markets, substantial damage could have been inflicted on many market participants . . . and could have potentially impaired the economies of many nations, including our own."

• • •

James Leach, the chairman of the banking committee and a long-time fan of Greenspan, responded by saying that the United States had lost "moral authority" in the world as a result of the Fed's rescue.

"The Fed's intervention comes at a time when our government has been preaching to foreign governments, especially Asian ones, that the way to modernize is to let weak institutions fail and rely on market mechanisms rather than insider bailouts."

—"Private-sector Refinancing of the Large Hedge Fund, Long-Term Capital Management"; before the Committee on Banking and Financial Services, U.S. House of Representatives; October 1, 1998

# Greenspan on:
# Education

I n light of the vast technological changes coming forth and the increasing sophistication of our marketplace, Greenspan promotes the need to upgrade people's skills both on and off the job. His main concern is that, without the proper education, not only will individuals fall behind their peers, but the United States, as a nation, will find itself no longer in the economic lead on many burgeoning technologies.

In the long run, companies are better off training their workers and increasing their skill base, than continuing to bid up the price for a limited number of skilled workers from an ever-diminishing labor pool.

"As output increasingly embodies ideas, labor force adaptation requires education. Not surprisingly, there has been a trend toward rising relative wages for those with higher levels of education. During the past fifteen years, the earnings of college graduates have increased relative to those who are high school graduates and, in turn, high school graduates have continued to open up their advantage over those who are high school dropouts. In fact, an increasing minority of our labor force has experienced real wage decreases, and surely this fact has accentuated unease, despite increases in living standards, on average, for our populace.

"Clearly, we must focus on ways to improve the skills and earning power of those who appear to be falling behind. We need to raise the supply of better educated workers if the recent trend toward rising wage dispersion is to be contained. In the long run, better child-rearing and better schools are essential. But in the shorter run, on-the-job training is a critical necessity—to overcome the educational deficiencies of all too many of our young people, and to renew the skills of workers who have fallen behind the rapidly rising curve of technological change. It has become quite apparent that many firms have concluded that it makes more sense to invest in such training than to bid up wage scales in a zero-sum competition for the existing limited pool of well-qualified workers. The bottom line, though, as I indicated earlier, is that individuals are going to have to be prepared to maintain skills as new procedures and equipment become part of a rapidly evolving economy."

—BEFORE THE ECONOMIC CLUB OF CHICAGO, CHICAGO; OCTOBER 19, 1995

• • •

With all the emphasis on technology—although well meaning and indeed necessary—Greenspan warns that colleges should not forget liberal arts education. For people to be creative in technological areas, they must also be versed in the liberal arts.

"Colleges and universities are being challenged to evaluate how new information technologies can best be employed in their curricula and their delivery systems. Beyond these more practical issues, the most significant challenge facing our universities is to ensure that teaching and research continue to unleash the creative intellectual energy that drives our system forward. As the conceptual share of the value added in our economic processes continues to grow, the ability to think abstractly will be increasingly important across a broad range of professions. Critical awareness and the abilities to hypothesize, to interpret, and to communicate are essential elements of successful innovation in a conceptual-based economy.

"The challenge for our institutions of higher education is to successfully blend the exposure to all aspects of human intellectual activity, especially our artistic propensities and our technical skills. What makes the challenge particularly daunting is that scientific knowledge expands and broadens the measurable rewards of its curriculum at a pace that liberal arts, by their nature, arguably have difficulty matching.

"Overwhelmed with the increasing scientific knowledge base, our universities are going to have to struggle to prevent the liberal arts curricula from being swamped by technology and science. It is crucial that that not happen."

—AT THE 81ST ANNUAL MEETING OF THE AMERICAN COUNCIL ON EDUCATION, WASHINGTON, D.C. ; FEBRUARY 16, 1999

"A liberal education was presumed in years past to produce a greater understanding of all aspects of living—an essential ingredient for broadening one's world view. I believe it still does. Viewing a great painting or listening to a profoundly moving piano concerto produces a sense of intellectual joy that is satisfying in and of itself. But, arguably, it also enhances and reinforces the conceptual processes so essential to innovation."

—COMMENCEMENT ADDRESS, HARVARD UNIVERSITY, CAMBRIDGE, MASSACHUSETTS; JUNE 10, 1999

• • •

Education must not stop once a person graduates from school. Workers must embrace a regimen of lifelong learning.

"Education is increasingly becoming a lifelong activity; businesses are now looking for employees who are prepared to continue learning, and workers and managers in many kinds of pursuits had better look forward to persistent hard work acquiring and maintaining the skills needed to cope with a dynamically evolving economy."

—AT THE BUILDING DEDICATION CEREMONIES AT THE KENAN-FLAGLER BUSINESS SCHOOL, UNIVERSITY OF NORTH CAROLINA, CHAPEL HILL; SEPTEMBER 12, 1997

• • •

Companies must take responsibility in offering resources for their employees to engage in on-the-job training. It benefits the employee and the employer alike.

"Firms and employees alike need to recognize that obtaining the potential rewards of the new technologies in the years ahead will require a renewed commitment to effective education and training, especially on-the-job training. Such a commitment is essential if we are to prevent the disruptions to lives and to the nation's capacity to produce that arise from mismatches between jobs and workers. We need to improve the preparation for the job market our schools do, but even better schools are unlikely to be able to provide adequate skills to support a lifetime of work. Indeed, ensuring that our labor force has the ongoing education and training necessary to compete in an increasingly sophisticated world economy is a critical task for the years ahead."

—BEFORE THE HOUSE COMMITTEE ON THE BUDGET; MARCH 27, 1996

# Greenspan on:

# Employment

W e are in the tightest job market in decades, a fallout of our growing economic prosperity. While this may be good news for workers who find themselves in demand, there is a downside to employers in the short term and the economy in the long term. Alan Greenspan is concerned that the ever-decreasing pool of skilled workers could spell the end of our economic growth. Without these workers, companies will not be able to expand; substituting capital for labor has limits. He has pondered many solutions to this problem and is a proponent of companies investing in their workers in the form of on-the-job training to ensure a steady supply of qualified employees. He has also called for more skills training in high schools and colleges.

---

Running out of skilled workers may eventually trigger inflation.

"Although productivity has accelerated in recent years, the impressive strength of domestic demand, in part driven by sharply rising equity prices, has meant that the substitution of capital for labor has been inadequate to prevent us from steadily depleting the pool of available workers.

"This worker depletion constitutes a critical upside risk to the inflation outlook because it presumably cannot continue without eventually putting increasing pressure on labor markets and on costs.

"Accelerating productivity may have appeared to break the link between labor market conditions and wage gains in recent years, but it cannot have changed the law of supply and demand.

"At some point, labor market conditions can become so tight that the rise in nominal wages will start increasingly outpacing the gains in labor productivity, and prices inevitably will then eventually begin to accelerate.

"Under those circumstances, inflation premiums embodied in long-term interest rates would doubtless rise. The attendant increased risk premiums would boost real interest rates as well, as investors become less certain about future price prospects."

—AT THE 35TH ANNUAL CONFERENCE ON BANK STRUCTURE AND COMPETITION OF THE FEDERAL RESERVE BANK OF CHICAGO, CHICAGO; MAY 6, 1999

• • •

Rapid changes in the work place are terrifying to many workers.

"As human intelligence appears without limit to engage our physical environment, human psychology remains, in some more primordial sense, invariant to time. The rapidity of change in our capital assets, the infrastructure with which all workers must interface day-by-day, has clearly raised the level of anxiety and insecurity in the workforce."

—AT THE 81ST ANNUAL MEETING OF THE AMERICAN COUNCIL ON EDUCATION, WASHINGTON, D.C.; FEBRUARY 16, 1999

• • •

Many workers, because of a lack of technical skills, are being left behind. They are frightened at their lowered prospects.

"There is also little doubt that this transition to the new high-tech economy, of which rising trade is a part, is proving difficult for a large segment of our workforce that interfaces with our rapidly changing capital stock day-by-day.

". . . Moreover, while major advances in standards of living are evident among virtually all nations that have opened their borders to increased competition, the adjustment trauma has also distressed those who once thrived in companies that were then at the cutting edge of technology, but which have since become increasingly less competitive in both domestic and foreign markets. Economists will say that workers should move from the steel districts of western Pennsylvania to a vibrant Silicon Valley. And eventually they, or more likely, their children, will. But the adjustment process is wrenching to an existing workforce made redundant largely through no fault of their own. It may be argued that all workers should have the foresight to recognize shifts in long-term job opportunities and move in advance of obsolescence. This regrettably is a skill not in great abundance—among business managers or the economists who counsel them, as well as among workers."

—"TRADE AND TECHNOLOGY"; BEFORE THE MINNESOTA MEETING, MINNEAPOLIS; SEPTEMBER 30, 1999

"It is one thing to believe that the economy, indeed the job market, will do well overall but quite another to feel secure about one's individual situation, given the accelerated pace of corporate restructuring and the heightened fear of skill obsolescence that has apparently characterized this expansion."

—*The Federal Reserve's Semiannual Monetary Policy Report;* before
the Committee on Banking, Housing, and Urban Affairs,
U.S. Senate; July 22, 1997

"In the short run, the fallout from rapidly changing technology is an environment in which the stock of plant and equipment with which most managers and workers interact is turning over increasingly rapidly, rendering a perception that human skills are becoming obsolete at a rate perhaps unprecedented in American history."

—at the Building Dedication Ceremonies at the Kenan-Flagler
Business School, University of North Carolina, Chapel Hill;
September 12, 1997

• • •

In previous years Greenspan might have suggested plastics to young grads. Now, it's finance.

"The advent of computer and telecommunications technology has spawned a vast proliferation of new financial derivatives products crafted by mathematicians and finance technicians who had never previously found favor on either Wall or Lombard streets. The above-average earnings they receive reflect the increasing value added created by financial institutions, which, in turn, results from their enhanced ability to marshal savings to support investment in the most productive physical capital."

—before the Annual Convention of the American Society of
Newspaper Editors, Washington, D.C.; April 2, 1998

"Businesses are now looking for employees who are prepared to continue learning. Linkages between business and education should be encouraged at all levels of our education system."

—AT THE BUILDING DEDICATION CEREMONIES AT THE KENAN-FLAGLER
BUSINESS SCHOOL, UNIVERSITY OF NORTH CAROLINA, CHAPEL HILL;
SEPTEMBER 12, 1997

• • •

Although companies can easily move employees around to capitalize on their talents, this short-term fix does nothing to increase the overall labor pool.

"Technology and management changes have had only a limited effect on the ability of *labor* supply to respond to changes in demand. To be sure, individual firms have acquired additional flexibility through increased use of outsourcing and temporary workers. In addition, smaller work teams may be able to adapt more readily to variations in order flows. While these techniques put the right workers at the right spots to reduce bottlenecks, they do not increase the aggregate supply of labor. That supply is sensitive to changes in demand but to a far more limited extent than facilities. New plants can almost always be built. But labor capacity for an individual country is constrained by the size of the working-age population, which, except for immigration, is basically determined several decades in the past. Its lead time reflects biology, not technology."

—BEFORE THE COMMITTEE ON THE BUDGET, U.S. HOUSE OF
REPRESENTATIVES; OCTOBER 8, 1997

"The debate about whether the introduction of technology would upgrade or 'deskill' the workforce is as old as Adam Smith. Certainly, one can point to some very routine types of jobs, such as those for telephone operators, that have lower skill requirements in today's world of automated communications systems than when more labor-intensive manual phone systems were in place. But, on the whole, the evidence suggests that across a wide range of industries, employers have upgraded their skill mix. Importantly, these changes represent not simply a shift in the occupational mix, but, to a larger degree, an upgrading of skill requirements of individual jobs for which the range and complexity of tasks and the scope for problem-solving and decision-making has expanded."

—AT THE UNIVERSITY OF CONNECTICUT, STORRS; OCTOBER 14, 1997

• • •

Companies must make an investment in their workers if they and the company are to succeed.

"To be fully effective in achieving potential productivity improvements, technological innovations also require a considerable amount of human investment on the part of workers who have to deal with these devices on a day-to-day basis. On this score, we still may not have progressed very far. Many workers still possess only rudimentary skills in manipulating advanced information technology. In these circumstances, firms and employees alike need to recognize that obtaining the potential rewards of the new technologies in the years ahead will require a renewed commitment to effective education and training, especially on-the-job training. This is especially the case if we are to prevent the disruptions to lives and the nation's capacity to produce that arise from mismatches between jobs and workers. We need to improve the preparation for the job market our schools do, but even better schools are unlikely to be able to provide adequate skills to support a lifetime of work. Indeed, the need to ensure that our labor force has the ongoing education and training necessary to compete in an increasingly sophisticated world economy is a critical task for the years ahead."

—BEFORE THE COMMITTEE ON BANKING, HOUSING, AND URBAN AFFAIRS, U.S. SENATE; FEBRUARY 20, 1996

"If we are able to boost our investment in people, ideas, and processes as well as machines, the economy can operate more effectively as it adapts to change. This holds the potential to create an even greater payoff of a broadly based rise in living standards over the longer run."

—"MEETING THE FUTURE WITH BETTER EDUCATION," EDITORIAL/OPINION; *JOURNAL OF COMMERCE,* SEPTEMBER 17, 1997

• • •

Greenspan suggests that we study immigration as a means of increasing the pool of skilled and semiskilled workers.

"Not only in high-tech and in the farm area but throughout the country, aggregate demand is putting pressure on an ever-decreasing supply of unemployed labor. One obvious means one can use to offset that is expanding the number of people we allow in, either generally or in focused areas. I think an appraisal of our immigration policies in this regard is on the table. I recognize there are huge problems associated with that, such as the question of the social safety net we have in this country, which is very substantial. It would be obviously inappropriate to open up our immigration capabilities to people who did not come to work. But all the experience that I've seen suggests that people seeking to come to the United States are coming for jobs and the opportunities we have here. I don't therefore perceive that as more than a theoretical problem. So I think that reviewing our immigration laws in the context of the type of economy that we will be enjoying in the decade ahead is clearly on the table."

—BEFORE THE SENATE BANKING COMMITTEE; JANUARY 26, 2000

"While immigration and imports can significantly cushion the consequences of the wealth effect [increased value of equities] and its draining of the pool of unemployed workers for a while, there are limits. Immigration is constrained by law and its enforcement; imports, by the willingness of global investors to accumulate dollar assets; and the drawdown of the pool of workers by the potential emergence of inflationary imbalances in labor markets. Admittedly, we are groping to infer where those limits may be. But that there are limits cannot be open to question.

". . . To be sure, increases in wages in excess of productivity growth may not be inflationary, and destructive of economic growth, if offset by decreases in other costs or declining profit margins. A protracted decline in margins, however, is a recipe for recession. Thus, if our objective of maximum sustainable economic growth is to be achieved, the pool of available workers cannot shrink indefinitely."

—"TECHNOLOGY AND THE ECONOMY"; BEFORE THE ECONOMIC CLUB OF NEW YORK, NEW YORK CITY; JANUARY 13, 2000

• • •

One reason why Europe has not shared in as great a prosperity as the United States is the difficulty in dismissing workers.

"The high rates of return offered by the newer technologies are largely the result of labor cost displacement, and because it is more costly to dismiss workers in Europe and Japan, the rate of return on the same equipment is correspondingly less there than in the United States. Here, labor displacement is more readily countenanced both by law and by culture, facilitating the adoption of technology that raises standards of living over time.

"There, of course, has been a substantial amount of labor-displacing investment in Europe to obviate expensive increased employment as their economies grow. But it is not clear to what extent such investment has been directed at reducing *existing* levels of employment. It should always be remembered that in economies where dismissing a worker is expensive, hiring one will also be perceived to be expensive."

—"Technology and the Economy"; before the Economic Club of New York, New York City; January 13, 2000

# Greenspan on:
# The Federal Reserve

One of Greenspan's jobs is to continually make sure that Congress and the public understand the role of his agency. Often, he must defend the Fed against criticism that it has too heavy a hand on the economic throttle while at other times people believe that it is not doing enough. The Fed has been under fire also by those who think it makes too many vital decisions for a body of unelected public officials.

The Federal Reserve is the central bank of the United States, founded by Congress in 1913 to provide the nation with a safer, more flexible, and more stable monetary and financial system. In the Fed's own words, its duties fall into four general areas: (1) conducting the nation's monetary policy; (2) supervising and regulating banking institutions and protecting the credit rights of consumers; (3) maintaining the stability of the financial system; and (4) providing certain financial services to the U.S. government, the public, financial institutions, and foreign official institutions.

The law is specific about the Fed's role, but it has a wide latitude in how to accomplish it. Although much of the Fed's "look" was handed down by Greenspan's predecessor, Paul Volcker, Greenspan has put his mark on its style by making it less secretive and more focused on maintaining price stability.

"The appropriate role of a central bank in a democratic society is an important and controversial issue. The performance of such an institution has profound implications for the nation's economy and the people's standard of living. Americans have pondered the question of the appropriate role and structure for the central bank at length, beginning with the debate over the First Bank of the United States, which George Washington signed into existence in 1791."

—BEFORE THE COMMITTEE ON
BANKING, FINANCE, AND URBAN AFFAIRS,
U.S. HOUSE OF REPRESENTATIVES; OCTOBER 13, 1993

• • •

Even though its actions, such as changing interest rates, often impact the stock market, the Fed has no regulatory control over the market. That's the job of the Securities and Exchange Commission. Indeed, Greenspan believes that neither the Fed nor anyone else should control the market. Only investors (for better or worse ) should decide where the markets go.

"Preemptive policymaking requires that the Federal Reserve continually monitor economic conditions, update forecasts, and appraise the setting of its policy instrument. Equity prices figure importantly in that forecasting process because they influence aggregate demand. As I testified last month, the central bank cannot effectively directly target stock or other asset prices. Should an asset bubble arise, or even if one is already in train, monetary policy properly calibrated can doubtless mitigate at least part of the impact on the economy. And, obviously, if we could find a way to prevent or deflate emerging bubbles, we would be better off. But identifying a bubble in the process of inflating may be among the most formidable challenges confronting a central bank, pitting its own assessment of fundamentals against the combined judgment of millions of investors."

—"The Federal Reserve's Semiannual Report on Monetary Policy"; before the Committee on Banking and Financial Services, U.S. House of Representatives; July 22, 1999

• • •

Greenspan believes a stitch in time saves nine. He has been criticized for taking action before problems arise. He counters by saying that the Fed's job is to head off problems rather than deal with them once they appear. If it waits too long, the cure can be worse than the disease.

"For monetary policy to foster maximum sustainable economic growth, it is useful to preempt forces of imbalance before they threaten economic stability.

". . . When we can be preemptive, we should be, because modest preemptive actions can obviate the need of more drastic actions at a later date."

—before a Joint Economic Committee of Congress; June 17, 1999

"If the Federal Reserve waits until actual inflation worsens before taking counter-measures, it would have waited far too long. At that point, modest corrective steps would no longer be enough to contain emerging economic imbalances and to avoid a buildup of inflation expectations and a significant backup of long-term interest rates. Instead, more wrenching measures would be needed, with unavoidable adverse side effects on near-term economic activity."

—"Humphrey-Hawkins, Monetary Policy Testimony and Report to the Congress"; February 22, 1994

• • •

Although central banks should not interfere in local financial issues, they should get involved in larger breakdowns as a backup to banks.

"The management of systemic risk is properly the job of the central banks. Individual banks should not be required to hold capital against the possibility of overall financial breakdown. Indeed, central banks, by their existence, appropriately offer a form of catastrophe insurance to banks against such events."

—BEFORE THE CONFERENCE ON CAPITAL REGULATION IN THE 21ST CENTURY, FEDERAL RESERVE BANK OF NEW YORK, NEW YORK CITY; FEBRUARY 26, 1998

• • •

Here, mainly talking about foreign central banks that operate under the whim of political leaders, Greenspan nonetheless never misses a chance to tout the importance of the Fed's independence from political considerations.

"Weak central banks also have been a contributor to crises. To effectively support a stable currency, central banks need to be independent, meaning that their monetary policy decisions are not subject to the dictates of political authorities."

—"RISK MANAGEMENT IN THE GLOBAL FINANCIAL SYSTEM"; BEFORE THE ANNUAL FINANCIAL MARKETS CONFERENCE OF THE FEDERAL RESERVE BANK OF ATLANTA, MIAMI BEACH, FLORIDA; FEBRUARY 27, 1998

• • •

After a half-hour walking tour of South-Central Los Angeles, Greenspan commented to reporters:

"We regulators are swamped with all sorts of data, which we pore through day after day. I think it's terribly important to look at what is under the data. It's important to put a face on the numbers."

—AT A COMMUNITY FORUM ON COMMUNITY REINVESTMENT AND ACCESS TO CREDIT: CALIFORNIA'S CHALLENGE, LOS ANGELES; JANUARY 12, 1998

• • •

The Fed walks a fine line between acting as a safety net for financial institution failures and letting the free market reign.

"Government intervention has been a mixed blessing. The federal safety net for banks clearly diminishes the effectiveness of private market regulation, creates perverse incentives for some banks to take excessive risk, and requires that we substitute more government supervision and regulation for the market discipline that played such an important role through much of our banking history."

—"OUR BANKING HISTORY"; BEFORE THE ANNUAL MEETING AND CONFERENCE OF THE CONFERENCE OF STATE BANK SUPERVISORS, NASHVILLE, TENNESSEE; MAY 2, 1998

"I would argue that the first imperative when evaluating market regulation is to enunciate clearly the public policy objectives that government regulation would be intended to promote. What market characteristics do policymakers seek to encourage? Efficiency? Fair and open access? What phenomena do we wish to discourage or eliminate? Fraud, manipulation, or other unfair practices? Systemic instability? Without explicit answers to these questions, government regulation is unlikely to be effective. More likely, it will prove unnecessary, burdensome, and perhaps even contrary to what more careful consideration would reveal to be the underlying objectives."

—AT THE FINANCIAL MARKETS CONFERENCE OF THE FEDERAL RESERVE BANK OF ATLANTA, CORAL GABLES, FLORIDA; FEBRUARY 21, 1997

"The objectives of the central bank in crisis management are to contain financial losses and prevent a contagious loss of confidence so that difficulties at one institution do not spread more widely to others. The focus of its concern is not to avoid the failure of entities that have made poor decisions or have had bad luck, but rather to see that such failures—or threats of failures—do not have broad and serious impacts on financial markets and the national, and indeed the global, economy."

—BEFORE THE SUBCOMMITTEE ON CAPITAL MARKETS,
SECURITIES AND GOVERNMENT SPONSORED ENTERPRISES
OF THE COMMITTEE ON BANKING AND FINANCIAL SERVICES,
U.S. HOUSE OF REPRESENTATIVES; MARCH 19, 1997

• • •

The Fed's main contribution to long-term growth is to maintain low inflation rates.

"In my view, improving productivity and standards of living necessitates increasing incentives to risk-taking. To encourage people to take prudent risks, the potential rewards must be perceived to exceed the possible losses. Maintaining low inflation rates reduces the levels of future uncertainties and, hence, increases the scope of investment opportunities. It is here that the Federal Reserve can most contribute to long-term growth."

—AT THE 1997 HASKINS PARTNERS DINNER OF THE STERN SCHOOL OF
BUSINESS, NEW YORK UNIVERSITY, NEW YORK CITY; MAY 8, 1997

• • •

The Fed must pay attention to even the most subtle data offered by markets.

"Whenever possible, regulators should use approaches to regulation and supervision that include or simulate market techniques and signals."
—AT THE CHICAGO FEDERAL RESERVE BANK CONFERENCE ON BANK STRUCTURE AND COMPETITION; MAY 2, 1996

• • •

Part of Greenspan's brilliance as an economist is that he knows that data and statistics go just so far. At some point, experience and judgment about risks play a part in any decision.

"In order to realize the benefits of low and declining inflation, Federal Reserve policy has, for some time now, been designed to act preemptively—as I indicated earlier—to look beyond current data readings and base action on its assessment of where the economy is headed.

"We must never forget that no matter how technologically complex our supervisory systems become, the basic unit of supervision on which all else rests remains the human judgment of the degree of risk."
—AT THE FEDERATION OF BANKERS ASSOCIATIONS OF JAPAN, TOKYO; NOVEMBER 18, 1996

"A healthy mix of two techniques is used in economic forecasting at the Federal Reserve. Model-based results often provide a useful starting point for framing the overall outlook. They also help us to gauge quickly the likely influence of incoming information on the outlook and to estimate the sensitivity of forecasts to key conditioning assumptions. However, in spite of the usefulness of models, the role of judgment remains substantial. For example, a significant degree of judgment must be used when reconciling results from a variety of formal, econometric equations, all of which have some degree of plausibility as representations of economic behavior. Moreover, incorporating anecdotal evidence, which may reveal important economic changes before they are reflected in any data, can only be accomplished judgmentally. In that regard, the Federal Reserve benefits substantially from the timely information reported by the District Banks from their extensive contacts with businesses within their regions. Given the tremendous quantity of data with which we are faced—much of it of an idiosyncratic nature—and given the changing economic environment and institutions, the Federal Reserve relies heavily on judgment in evaluating economic prospects."

—BEFORE THE 32ND ANNUAL MEETING OF THE NATIONAL ASSOCIATION OF BUSINESS ECONOMISTS, WASHINGTON, D.C.; SEPTEMBER 23–27, 1990

• • •

Under Greenspan, the Fed has assumed a more open stance. Beginning in January 2000, the Fed said, it would release a statement at the end of every meeting explaining Fed thoughts on inflation dangers even if the session did not result in an interest rate change. In the past few years, it had also begun a program of mentioning its "bias" on interest rate changes.

"If we are to maintain the confidence of the American people, it is vitally important that, excepting the certain areas where the premature release of information could frustrate our legislated mission, the Fed must be as transparent as any agency of government. It cannot be acceptable in a democratic society that a group of unelected individuals are vested with important responsibilities, without being open to full public scrutiny and accountability.

"At the heart of this issue is balance: The appropriate degree of openness comes from striking the right balance between the public's right to know and the need for effective policymaking and implementation.

". . . As a general matter, it is desirable for public institutions to conduct their business in the open. The Federal Reserve endorses this principle and adheres to it, except when doing so would prevent us from fulfilling our fundamental mission of producing sound public policy. Holding open meetings of the FOMC [Federal Open Market Committee] or releasing a videotape, audiotape, or transcript of them would so seriously constrain the process of formulating policy as to render those meetings nearly unproductive. The candid airing of views, the forthright give and take, and the tentative posing of new ideas likely would disappear. Monetary policy would suffer and the economy with it."

—AT THE ANNUAL DINNER AND FRANCIS BOYER LECTURE OF THE AMERICAN ENTERPRISE INSTITUTE FOR PUBLIC POLICY RESEARCH, WASHINGTON, D.C.; DECEMBER 5, 1996

"We have also learned that the Federal Reserve's potential contributions to financial and economic stability should not end with making policy decisions. We also need to explain to the public what we are doing and why. Importantly, in our democratic system our explanations provide the members of this Committee, your Congressional colleagues, and the people you serve with the information necessary to evaluate our actions and to hold us accountable for them. As you know, we have made considerable efforts in recent years to improve the communication of our decisions, our expectations, and their rationales to the public consistent with our mandate to deliver effective monetary policy. This has not always been a straightforward process, in which the consequences of each step could be readily predicted, but it is one that must continue."

—BEFORE THE U.S. SENATE BANKING COMMITTEE; JANUARY 26, 2000

"More often, the Federal Reserve judges that policy implementation is better served through small, incremental operating moves that do not connote a significant alternation in policy intent and do not have major implications for financial conditions in the more distant future. Signaling such policy moves through open market operations usually avoids major and potentially destabilizing movements in bond and stock prices.

"This way of distinguishing the nature of policy intent may well convey information to the financial markets about the future direction of policy better than would a formal, immediate announcement of every policy change."

—BEFORE THE COMMITTEE ON BANKING, HOUSING, AND URBAN AFFAIRS, U.S. SENATE; FEBRUARY 22, 1990

• • •

Greenspan has said many times that no one can stop a recession or any other economic downturn. However, he sees the Fed's role as one of preventing deep recessions and monumental catastrophes.

"Policymaking is an uncertain enterprise. Monetary policy actions work slowly and incrementally by affecting the decisions of millions of households and businesses. And we adjust policy step by step as new information becomes available on the effects of previous actions and on the economic background against which policy will be operating. No individual step is ever likely to be decisive in pushing the economy or prices one way or another—there is no monetary policy 'straw that broke the camel's back.' The cumulative effects of many policy actions may be substantial, but the historical record suggests that any given change in rates will have about the same effect as a previous change of the same size.

"Because the effects of monetary policy are felt only slowly and with a lag, policy will have a better chance of contributing to meeting the nation's macroeconomic objectives if we look forward as we act—however indistinct our view of the road ahead.

"The Federal Reserve has no magical power to eliminate economic fluctuations. But we endeavor to minimize them, and in doing so, seek to improve the environment for long-term economic growth."

—BEFORE THE BOARD OF DIRECTORS, NATIONAL ASSOCIATION OF REALTORS, WASHINGTON, D.C.; MAY 16, 1995

"One of the Federal Reserve's principal objectives in its capacity as a bank supervisory agency is to promote a sound, competitive, and innovative banking system—a system that can effectively provide credit and other important banking services within the context of a strong and stable economy."

—BEFORE THE COMMITTEE ON SMALL BUSINESS, U.S. HOUSE OF REPRESENTATIVES; JUNE 6, 1990

•  •  •

Here, Greenspan seems to take almost full responsibility for fighting inflation. It wasn't until a few years later that he said that Congress must do its duty in lowering inflation by lowering the budget deficit.

"The principal role of monetary policy is to provide a stable backdrop against which economic decisions can be made. In the long run, the link between money and prices is unassailable. That link is central to the mission of the Federal

Reserve, for it reminds us that, without the acquiescence of the central bank, inflation cannot take root.

"Ultimately, the monetary authorities must face the responsibility for lasting price trends. While oil-price shocks, droughts, higher taxes, or new government regulations may boost price indexes at one time or another, sustained inflation requires at least the forbearance of the central bank."

—BEFORE THE HOUSE SUBCOMMITTEE ON DOMESTIC MONETARY POLICY;
JULY 20, 1989

• • •

Greenspan seems to change his view when he says that Congress must do its part in stemming inflation by dealing with the budget deficit.

"Monetary policy is only one tool, and it cannot be used successfully to meet multiple objectives. The Federal Reserve, for example, can address itself to either domestic prices or exchange rates but cannot be expected to achieve objectives for both simultaneously. Monetary policy alone is not readily capable of addressing today's large current account deficit, which is symptomatic of underlying imbalances among saving, spending, and production within the U.S. economy. Continued progress in reducing the federal deficit is a more appropriate instrument to raise domestic saving and free additional resources for productive investment. The long-term health of our economy requires the balanced use of monetary and fiscal policy to reach all of the nation's policy objectives."

—BEFORE THE COMMITTEE ON BANKING, HOUSING,
AND URBAN AFFAIRS, U.S. SENATE; FEBRUARY 22, 1990

Q. Is it clear that the U.S. has not yet figured out how to eliminate the ups and downs of the business cycle?

A. We will, from time to time, have adjustments in the economy. They need not be particularly large. What a recession tends to do is unwind imbalances. Mild imbalances can be unwound with marginal effect upon production and employment. They are not built into the economy. They are caused by mistakes—most of all, the mistakes of Government policy.

—"Why Business Will Continue on the Upswing," Interview with
Alan Greenspan, Chairman, Council of Economic Advisors;
*U.S. News & World Report,* June 28, 1976

• • •

While never changing his belief that price stability is paramount, Greenspan knows that the Fed must be flexible in handling issues.

"The Federal Reserve must be willing to adjust its instruments fairly flexibly as these judgments evolve. We must not hesitate to reverse course occasionally if warranted by new developments. To be sure, we should not overreact to every bit of new information, because the frequent observations for a variety of economic statistics are subject to considerable transitory 'noise.' But we need to be willing to respond to indications of changing underlying economic trends, without losing sight of the ultimate policy objectives.

"To the extent that the underlying economic trends are judged to be deviating from a path consistent with reaching the ultimate objectives, the Federal Reserve would need to make 'midcourse' policy corrections. Such deviations from the appropriate direction for the economy will be inevitable, given the delayed and imperfectly predictable nature of the effects of previous policy actions. Numerous unforeseen forces not related to monetary policy will continue to buffet the economy. The limits of monetary policy in short-run stabilization need to be borne in mind.

"The business cycle cannot be repealed, but I believe it can be significantly damped by appropriate policy action. Price stability cannot be dictated by fiat, but governmental decision makers can establish the conditions needed to approach this goal over the next several years."

—BEFORE THE SENATE COMMITTEE ON BANKING, HOUSING, AND URBAN AFFAIRS; JULY 13, 1988

• • •

Greenspan was asked by Dennis Weatherstone, president of J. P. Morgan & Co., if the central bank's job "was more of an art than a science."

"We hope it remains something of a science rather than this mystic endeavor that never seems to work," said Greenspan.

—IN A QUESTION-AND-ANSWER SESSION WITH MEMBERS OF THE ECONOMIC CLUB OF NEW YORK, NEW YORK CITY; JUNE 14, 1988

• • •

Timing is everything.

"I cannot rule out a policy mistake as the trigger for a downturn. We at the Federal Reserve might fail to restrain a speculative surge in the economy or fail to recognize that we were holding reserves too tight for too long. Given the lags in the effects of policy, forecasts inevitably are involved and thus errors inevitably arise. Our job is to keep such errors to an absolute minimum. An efficient policy is one that doesn't lose its bearings, that homes in on price stability over time, but that copes with and makes allowances for any unforeseen weakness in economic activity. It is such a policy that the Federal Reserve will endeavor to pursue."

—BEFORE THE COMMITTEE ON BANKING, HOUSING, AND URBAN AFFAIRS, U.S. SENATE; AUGUST 1, 1989

"Monetary policy works with considerable lags, and waiting until inflation picks up risks a boom-and-bust economic cycle inimical to business and household planning, to saving and investment, and to the longer-term growth of the U.S. economy. As I indicated to the Congress in testimony earlier this year, the hallmark of a successful monetary policy will be an inflation rate that does not rise."

—BEFORE THE JOINT ECONOMIC COMMITTEE, U.S. CONGRESS; DECEMBER 7, 1994

"We recognize that estimates of the economy's potential are just that—estimates, subject to the considerable uncertainties attached to all economic estimates. In setting monetary policy, the Federal Reserve is looking to encourage the highest level of activity that the economy can sustain, not to hold it back. We would welcome the possibility that our economic performance can be in excess of historical relationships."

—BEFORE THE JOINT ECONOMIC COMMITTEE, U.S. CONGRESS; DECEMBER 7, 1994

• • •

Greenspan understands that the Fed's success is preventing what "didn't" occur. That, of course, is impossible to measure or prove.

"As the nation's central bank, the Federal Reserve stands at the nexus of monetary policy, supervisory policy, and the payments system. Part of our task is to minimize the risk of systemic crises while endeavoring to implement a macroeconomic policy that supports maximum sustainable economic growth. When, for example, threats to the nation's financial system loomed large in the wake of the 1987 stock market crash, the Federal Reserve effectively contained the secondary consequences of the crash with prompt but prudent injections of liquidity and with constant consultations with depository institutions during the crisis. The bulk of our efforts in this area, however, of necessity garners considerably less publicity, as it is directed at ongoing efforts to fend off financial sector problems before those problems emerge as full-blown crises that could threaten American jobs and living standards. Much of our success over the years, therefore, reflects crises that did not happen. In working with other regulatory agencies, the Federal Reserve has also brought its broad perspective to bear on supervisory actions that could have had macroeconomic or monetary policy implications."

—BEFORE THE COMMITTEE ON BANKING, FINANCE, AND URBAN AFFAIRS, U.S. HOUSE OF REPRESENTATIVES; OCTOBER 13, 1993

• • •

Raising interest rates is never an easy decision.

"A driver might tap the brakes to make sure not to be hit by a truck coming down a street, even if he thinks the chances of such an event are relatively low. The costs of being wrong are too high. In conducting monetary policy, the Federal Reserve needs constantly to look down the road to gauge the future risks to the economy and act accordingly."

—"THE FEDERAL RESERVE'S SEMIANNUAL MONETARY POLICY REPORT"; BEFORE THE COMMITTEE ON BANKING, HOUSING, AND URBAN AFFAIRS, U.S. SENATE; JULY 22, 1997

"A central bank's raising interest rates is rarely popular. But the Federal Reserve's action on March 25, 1997 to tighten the stance of monetary policy, seems to have attracted more than the usual share of attention and criticism. . . .

"Even if it should appear in retrospect that we could have skirted the dangers of credit excesses without a modest tightening, the effect on the expansion would be small, temporary, and like most insurance, its purchase to protect against possible adverse outcomes would still be eminently sensible.

"For the Federal Reserve to remain inactive against a possible buildup of insidious inflationary pressures would be to sanction a threat to the job security and standards of living of too many Americans."

—AT THE 1997 HASKINS PARTNERS DINNER OF THE STERN SCHOOL OF BUSINESS, NEW YORK UNIVERSITY, NEW YORK CITY; MAY 8, 1997

• • •

The Fed is a growing, ever-changing, and maturing institution.

"In practice, the central bank of the United States works, and it works well. On paper, however, its structure can appear unwieldy—an amalgam of regional and centralized authority and of public and private interests. If we were constructing a central bank for the United States now, starting from scratch, would it be identical to the Federal Reserve System described in current law? Perhaps not. But the Federal Reserve has evolved to be well suited to today's policy tasks.

"One of the reasons why the Federal Reserve is effective is that its basic structure has been in place for a long time. The institution has been able to take that framework as a given and to adapt and build on it during decades of invaluable experience in the financial and economic setting of this country."

—BEFORE THE COMMITTEE ON BANKING, FINANCE, AND URBAN AFFAIRS, U.S. HOUSE OF REPRESENTATIVES; OCTOBER 13, 1993

# Greenspan on:
# Forecasting

---

**W**ithout question, Greenspan is one of the world's best economic forecasters. Despite the flood of information and data pored over by the Fed, he is the first to admit how little we know about making predictions. In the final analysis, experience, judgment, and guesswork play a large role in forecasting.

---

"There is little reason to believe that we are going to be any better at this [forecasting] in the future than in the past. Hence, despite the remarkable progress witnessed to date, we have to be quite modest about our ability to project the future of technology and its implications for productivity growth and for the broader economy."
—"THE AMERICAN ECONOMY IN A WORLD CONTEXT"; AT THE 35TH ANNUAL CONFERENCE ON BANK STRUCTURE AND COMPETITION OF THE FEDERAL RESERVE BANK OF CHICAGO, CHICAGO; MAY 6, 1999

"There is a very legitimate concern at this particular point about where the economy is heading. And I don't think anybody knows for sure."
—BEFORE THE COMMITTEE ON BANKING, HOUSING, AND URBAN AFFAIRS, U.S. SENATE; JULY 18, 1996

"As a practical matter, monetary policy cannot and should not be directed at a single forecast. We do not have the capability, nor does anyone else, to be able to know with certainty precisely where the economy is going to be."

—BEFORE THE COMMITTEE ON BANKING, HOUSING,
AND URBAN AFFAIRS, U.S. SENATE; FEBRUARY 21, 1996

"In order to realize the benefits of low and declining inflation, Federal Reserve policy has, for some time now, been designed to act preemptively—as I indicated earlier—to look beyond current data readings and base action on its assessment of where the economy is headed."

—BEFORE THE COMMITTEE ON BANKING, HOUSING,
AND URBAN AFFAIRS, U.S. SENATE; JULY 18, 1996

"History is strewn with the most erudite scientists of earlier ages proffering forecasts of technological developments, which, in retrospect, seem incomprehensible in their degree of inaccuracy."

—AT THE 80TH ANNIVERSARY AWARDS DINNER OF THE
CONFERENCE BOARD, NEW YORK CITY; OCTOBER 16, 1996

• • •

The best tool for forecasting is modeling. The problem is knowing how to make the model.

"There is, regrettably, no simple model of the American economy that can effectively explain the levels of output, employment, and inflation. In principle, there may be some unbelievably complex set of equations that does that. But we have not been able to find them, and do not believe anyone else has either.

"Consequently, we are led, of necessity, to employ ad hoc partial models and intensive informative analysis to aid in evaluating economic developments and implementing policy. There is no alternative to this, though we continuously seek to enhance our knowledge to match the ever-growing complexity of the world economy."

—AT THE ANNUAL DINNER AND FRANCIS BOYER LECTURE OF THE
AMERICAN ENTERPRISE INSTITUTE FOR PUBLIC POLICY RESEARCH,
WASHINGTON, D.C.; DECEMBER 5, 1996

• • •

Monetary policy changes take time to work. Forecasting must take that lag time into account.

"Because monetary policy works with a lag, it is not the conditions prevailing today that are critical but rather those likely to prevail six to 12 months, or even longer, from now. Hence, as difficult as it is, we must arrive at some judgment about the most probable direction of the economy and the distribution of risks around that expectation."

—BEFORE THE COMMITTEE ON THE BUDGET,
U.S. SENATE; JANUARY 21, 1997

• • •

One factor that forecasters can count on is that information and ideas are replacing physical goods as a storehouse of wealth.

"Ancient soothsayers may have been able to penetrate the future, but unfortunately they chose to vouchsafe precious few tricks of their trade to today's central bankers. The most effective means we have for looking over the horizon is to try to identify which of the forces currently driving our economy are transitory and which are deep seated and likely to persist in the longer term.

"One major deep-seated force that we can identify with some assurance is the trend toward an increasing conceptual

content of output—the substitution, in effect, of ideas for physical matter in the creation of economic value."
—BEFORE THE ECONOMIC CLUB OF CHICAGO, CHICAGO; OCTOBER 19, 1995

"Breakthroughs in computing hardware, software, and communication technologies may allow data collection to be more precise, but these and other innovations make the economy more difficult to measure. This results, in large part, because output of goods and services is increasingly becoming more conceptual than physical overtime. The part of the real value of output that reflects ideas rather than bulk has increased immeasurably this century. As a consequence, the units of output have become ever more difficult to identify.

"One ton of 99.7 percent pure aluminum is fairly well defined with respect to quantity and quality. A computer program is not. Clearly, unless output is unambiguously defined, the concept of price is vague. Moreover, the conceptualization of output is one of the factors that has been associated with substantial increases in the quality of goods and services. Measurement of the extent of that improvement, quite obviously, is problematic, and, in turn, has critical implications for aggregate price indexes. Any imprecision in those calculations of prices translates directly into uncertainty in the real values of output and productivity."
—BEFORE THE COMMERCE, CONSUMER, AND MONETARY AFFAIRS COMMITTEE OF THE HOUSE COMMITTEE ON GOVERNMENT OPERATIONS; AUGUST 10, 1994

• • •

The effects of mergers are particularly difficult to forecast.

"We do not have and cannot have the resources required to fully understand the implications of mergers. Forecasting how markets or technologies will evolve is an excruciatingly difficult task. We sometimes do it reasonably well and sometimes we do it poorly."

—"The Effects of Mergers"; before the Committee on the Judiciary, U.S. Senate; June 16, 1998

• • •

Forecasters are often caught by surprise.

"We policymakers have been engaged in a lot of on-the-job training in recent years. The remarkable American economy, whose roots are still not known conclusively, and the Asian crises that caught us by surprise, among other humbling experiences, have made policymakers particularly sensitive to how fast the world can shift beneath our feet.

"We need to be alert to the dramatic changes that are confronting us continuously, but recognize that neither the fundamental laws of economics, nor human nature, on which they are based, has changed, or is likely to change.

"This will be an especially important notion to keep in mind as we continue to grapple with the rapidly changing global economic environment and its regulatory structure."

—"The American Economy in a World Context"; at the 35th Annual Conference on Bank Structure and Competition of the Federal Reserve Bank of Chicago, Chicago; May 6, 1999

"Can we project how long the economy of the United States can act as a buffer to weakness elsewhere? The answer: Not easily. History counsels us that sharp changes in direction are rarely, if ever, anticipated."

—at the 35th Annual Conference on Bank Structure and Competition of the Federal Reserve Bank of Chicago, Chicago; May 6, 1999

• • •

The lessons of history are not always repeated as we would expect.

"I wish it were possible to lay out in advance exactly what conditions have to prevail to portend a buildup of inflation pressures or inflationary psychology. However, the circumstances that have been associated with increasing inflation in the past have not followed a single pattern. The processes have differed from cycle to cycle, and what may have been a useful leading indicator in one instance has given off misleading signals in another."

—"THE FEDERAL RESERVE'S SEMIANNUAL MONETARY POLICY REPORT";
BEFORE THE COMMITTEE ON BANKING, HOUSING, AND URBAN AFFAIRS,
U.S. SENATE; FEBRUARY 26, 1997

"Whether employed by the government or by private firms, it is vital that forecasters have a clear understanding of what economic events they are attempting to anticipate and over what time periods. Success in this effort requires a thorough knowledge of how the focus of the forecast relates to the objectives of the decisionmaker and reflects the critical features of the economic environment in which he or she must operate. Too often one observes forecasts that seem to focus on a set of economic statistics because they are readily available or the traditional object of analysis, rather than because of their immediate relevance to the decisionmaker The adept forecaster is capable of drawing the distinction."

—BEFORE THE 32ND ANNUAL MEETING OF THE NATIONAL ASSOCIATION OF
BUSINESS ECONOMISTS, WASHINGTON, D.C.; SEPTEMBER 23–27, 1990

• • •

Doing the forecasting legwork is only part of the job. How that knowledge is presented to the consumer is equally important.

"In both the private and public sectors, a large gap commonly exists between the expectations of consumers of forecasts and the abilities of the forecaster. In some cases the forecaster must overcome considerable skepticism that economic projections are of any value. In other cases, expectations reach far beyond the abilities of the practitioner. In either situation, the clarity with which the forecaster can communicate the key conditioning assumptions and the uncertainties surrounding a forecast can be as important as the predictions themselves."
—BEFORE THE 32ND ANNUAL MEETING OF THE NATIONAL ASSOCIATION OF
    BUSINESS ECONOMISTS, WASHINGTON, D.C.; SEPTEMBER 23–27, 1990

• • •

Human judgment is still necessary.

"There are limits to the apparent power of the econometric model as a forecasting tool. In spite of significant progress toward accommodating more sophisticated—and we hope more realistic formal models, it is still fair to say that, on the whole, our econometric models are at best very crude approximations of the true economy. The economy we are attempting to model is exceedingly complex, best characterized by continually evolving institutions and economic relationships. The widespread use of addfactors in most model-based projections is the clearest manifestation of the difficulty that our large-scale models have in representing a complicated reality. At this stage in their development, statistical models still require large doses of judgment if they are to be useful to decisionmakers."

—BEFORE THE 32ND ANNUAL MEETING OF THE NATIONAL ASSOCIATION OF BUSINESS ECONOMISTS, WASHINGTON, D.C.; SEPTEMBER 23–27, 1990

• • •

"For the most part, the strengths of intuitive forecasting complement the weaknesses of model-based prediction. The flexibility of the intuitive approach may allow its practitioner to adjust more quickly to shifts in key parameters or to perceived changes in the economic structure. At times of rapid change, such as at business cycle turning points, intuitive forecasters may be able to pick up on and react to the nonlinear response of the economy better than those who are relying solely on conventional econometric models. Moreover, intuitive forecasters may catch important developments early on by recognizing the signals or anomalies in weekly or monthly data as they are received. While some work has been done to formalize this process in statistical models, at present the judgmental forecaster seems to have the edge on this front.

"Given the strengths and weaknesses of these approaches, it seems obvious that the best forecasting strategy will incorporate features of both model-based and intuitive forecasting."

—BEFORE THE 32ND ANNUAL MEETING OF THE NATIONAL ASSOCIATION OF BUSINESS ECONOMISTS, WASHINGTON, D.C.; SEPTEMBER 23–27, 1990

• • •

You don't know where you're going, unless you know where you are.

"Detecting key imbalances is a crucial element in the forecast process and is one reason why determining where the economy is at any particular moment is so important in assessing where it may be headed. Much of a forecaster's success in predicting the future clearly depends on how well he or she can determine existing conditions. Given the difficulties we face in determining where we are at present, we should have only modest expectations for our ability to predict the future. While our forecasting tools have improved considerably over the postwar period, our forecast accuracy has not. This observation suggests that we are engaged in a continual struggle in which the benefits of improved techniques are eroded by an increasingly elusive and complex economic structure. Since inevitably the structure will become increasingly more complex in the years ahead, forecasters in both the private and public sectors face a constant challenge to develop more reliable forecast procedures that combine the flexibility of the intuitive approach with the systematic discipline of the model-based approach."

—BEFORE THE 32ND ANNUAL MEETING OF THE NATIONAL ASSOCIATION OF BUSINESS ECONOMISTS, WASHINGTON, D.C.; SEPTEMBER 23–27, 1990

• • •

Knowing that something will happen and when it will happen are two different forecasts. The latter is harder than the former.

"I should mention that 12 months is a rather long time for a forecast. All we as economists can do is forecast the development of the business cycle and its processes. We are much less adept at judging the time frame in which those events occur."

—"WHY BUSINESS WILL CONTINUE ON THE UPSWING," INTERVIEW WITH ALAN GREENSPAN, CHAIRMAN, COUNCIL OF ECONOMIC ADVISORS; *U.S. NEWS & WORLD REPORT,* JUNE 28, 1976

"I wish I could say that the business cycle has been repealed. But some day, some event will end the extraordinary string of economic advances that has prevailed since 1982."
—BEFORE THE HOUSE BANKING COMMITTEE'S SUBCOMMITTEE ON DOMESTIC MONETARY POLICY; JULY 21, 1989

"Forecasting inflation is a terribly complex issue. Saying one indicator is better than another is not very useful."
—AT THE 34TH ANNUAL INTERNATIONAL MONETARY CONFERENCE, CHICAGO; JUNE 8, 1988

• • •

Greenspan's forecasting record is among the best in the world, but he has had some amusing gaffes. Barbara Walters, whom he dated, tells how she took him to see an apartment that she was thinking of buying. She asked his opinion. "He advised me not to," she said. "We had the New York City fiscal crisis at the time, and I didn't buy it. The value has now tripled or quadrupled, so I tell Alan that now whenever he tells me not to buy a piece of real estate, I buy it."
—THE NEW YORK TIMES, JUNE 3, 1987

"The problem in forecasting is how to abstract from reality to a few relationships, maybe a thousand, that describe how the economy works. It's always an abstraction, and you're always asking yourself if you've got the right thousand."
—THE NEW YORK TIMES, JUNE 5, 1983

"The difficulty is that we have numbers that make the economy look reasonably good. But you determine the health of an economy not in a retrospective view. You look at the health of an economy in its forward dynamics. In other words, you would never argue that somebody who had an early incurable cancer was healthy, and yet he feels perfectly fine. But the prognosis is terrible.

"In the same sense, if interest rates and inflation stay up at these levels, the prognosis is terrible, because what we see is vast financial disruptions, terrible corporate liquidity problems."

—AT A MEETING WITH EDITORS AND REPORTERS,
*THE NEW YORK TIMES;* MARCH 24, 1981

• • •

Before making a forecast, economists must also determine what happens if their prognosis turns out wrong.

"In their efforts to understand the economy, analysts have tried to take advantage of new technology, including the manifold increase in computing power. Econometricians have devised complicated mathematical models that purport to describe relationships within the U.S. economy. Although these models serve many useful purposes, no matter how elaborate they may be, they are generally too simple to capture the evolving complexities of our economy. History teaches us that the underlying structure of the economy is in a continuing state of flux; current estimates of key parameters describing the basic relationships are based on past experience and need to be viewed skeptically when making policy for the future. As a consequence, alternative approaches to inferring the evolving structure of the economy are required.

"The appropriateness of monetary policy will depend on how successful we are in understanding the complex forces that are currently driving the economy. In the process of reaching such an understanding, we do not rely on a single, point forecast of economic activity. Instead, recognizing the uncertainty around any given forecast, we endeavor to look at a range of forecasts and to form judgments of their relative probabilities. Based on those judgments, we implement policy to meet national economic objectives. But we also recognize the inevitability of errors in forecasts. Policymaking requires an assessment of the consequences of various policy alternatives should they prove to be wrong. We must ask ourselves: How difficult would it be to reverse policy mistakes and at what cost?"

—"ON ECONOMIC FORECASTING"; BEFORE THE COMMERCE, CONSUMER, AND MONETARY AFFAIRS COMMITTEE OF THE HOUSE COMMITTEE ON GOVERNMENT OPERATIONS; AUGUST 10, 1994

"On balance, imprecision in the measurement of key economic magnitudes does complicate the job of policymaking. Making inferences about the future is always harder when readings on the economy are contaminated by measurement error. However, because of our ability to consult a variety of sources, the adverse effects of such mismeasurement are kept to a minimum. I am not aware that forecasting the U.S. economy is currently any more difficult or, for that matter, any easier than it was, say, several decades ago."

—"ON ECONOMIC FORECASTING"; BEFORE THE COMMERCE, CONSUMER, AND MONETARY AFFAIRS COMMITTEE OF THE HOUSE COMMITTEE ON GOVERNMENT OPERATIONS; AUGUST 10, 1994

"Having reflected on forecasting and economic statistics in the conduct of monetary policy, I remain confident in just one prediction: Future Federal Reserve chairmen will tell your successors on this panel that economic forecasting is still uncertain and that the consequences of monetary policy vary over time. The U.S. economy is complex and evolving. Keeping pace with that change will require our continuing efforts to understand how the economy works and to adapt our data-gathering procedures accordingly."

—"ON ECONOMIC FORECASTING"; BEFORE THE COMMERCE, CONSUMER, AND MONETARY AFFAIRS COMMITTEE OF THE HOUSE COMMITTEE ON GOVERNMENT OPERATIONS; AUGUST 10, 1994

"All policymakers recognize that notions of potential GDP growth and the natural rate of unemployment are considerable simplifications, useful in conceptual models but subject to a variety of real-world complications. Our economy is a complex, dynamic system, comprising countless and diverse households, firms, services, products, and prices, interacting in a multitude of markets. Estimates of macroeconomic relationships, as best we can make them, are useful starting points for analysis—but they are just starting points."

—BEFORE THE SENATE COMMITTEE ON BANKING, HOUSING, AND URBAN AFFAIRS; JULY 20, 1994

• • •

An upbeat prediction:

"It is my firm belief that, with fiscal consolidation and with the monetary policy path that we have charted, the United States is well positioned to remain at the forefront of the world economy well into the next century."

—BEFORE THE SUBCOMMITTEE ON ECONOMIC GROWTH AND CREDIT FORMATION OF THE COMMITTEE ON BANKING, FINANCE, AND URBAN AFFAIRS, U.S. HOUSE OF REPRESENTATIVES; JULY 20, 1993

• • •

The Fed relies on reports from all around the country to make its predictions more relevant to the nation as a whole.

"The strength of the institutions and structures of the Federal Reserve is perhaps most visible in the work of the Federal Open Market Committee. There, the ability of Reserve Bank presidents to draw on local contacts can reveal significant developments in the economy before they are visible in the national data, and can help in understanding the forces behind important economic trends. The Committee is

an extraordinary collection of individuals. Among the 17 people gathered around that table, 13 have PhDs. The others have the experience, skills, and common sense to prevent the Committee from becoming paralyzed with a surfeit of two-handed economists."
—BEFORE THE U.S. SENATE BANKING COMMITTEE; JANUARY 26, 2000

• • •

You can never know for sure what part of the business cycle you're in until it's over.

"It may be many years before we fully understand the nature of the rapid changes currently confronting our economy. We are unlikely to fully comprehend the process and its interactions with asset prices until we have been through a complete business cycle. Regrettably, we at the Federal Reserve do not have the luxury of awaiting a better set of insights into this process. Indeed, our goal, in responding to the complexity of current economic forces, is to extend the expansion by containing its imbalances and avoiding the very recession that would complete a business cycle.

"If we knew for sure that economic growth would soon be driven wholly by gains in productivity and growth of the working age population, including immigration, we would not need to be as concerned about the potential for infla-tionary distortions. Clearly, we cannot know for sure, because we are dealing with world economic forces which are new and untested."
—"TECHNOLOGY AND THE ECONOMY"; BEFORE THE ECONOMIC CLUB OF NEW YORK, NEW YORK CITY; JANUARY 13, 2000

# Greenspan on:

# The Gap Between Rich and Poor

W hile Greenspan's Fed has been hailed as bringing the longest-running era of prosperity in American history, not everyone has been sharing in the bounty. Although more families are moving up economically, anecdotally we know that the gap between rich and poor also has widened. Greenspan knows there is no quick fix, but he believes the answer is more education, the end of race and gender discrimination, and getting those in economic power to understand that if more people share in the wealth, then they, too, will benefit. He also believes that if inflation is kept in check, more people will see their standard of living increase no matter what level of the economy they reside in.

Greenspan rarely engages in emotional arguments to make his point. As much as he may find discrimination distasteful and immoral—and he has said so many times—he always couches the problem in economic terms. Here he shows how discrimination hurts everyone in our society from an economic point perspective. By hanging a price tag on discrimination, he hopes to help those in power to understand its terrible impact.

"Whether discrimination is a product of habit and culture, or the deliberate acts of individuals, the consequences are the same.

Unfair practices resulting in credit decisions that are not based on legitimate economic factors harm our society and impair our economy, not to mention reduce the profit opportunities of our banks. Discrimination in lending directly limits the ability of its victims to own homes, build businesses, credit job opportunities, or accumulate wealth. It stifles economic development and opportunity in our communities and neighborhoods. On a broader scale, discrimination in credit markets restricts the free flow of capital, reduces the demand for goods and services, and robs our economy of financial and human resources that can contribute to economic growth."

—BEFORE THE COMMITTEE ON BANKING, HOUSING,
AND URBAN AFFAIRS, U.S. SENATE; SEPTEMBER 22, 1994

• • •

Once a country is on sound economic ground, it must confront the issue of those who are not sharing in the wealth. To ignore this part of society is to sow the seeds of discontent and social instability.

"I believe that we as a people are very fortunate: When confronted with the choice between rapid growth with its inevitable insecurities and a stable, but stagnant economy, given time, Americans have chosen growth. But as we seek to manage what is now this increasingly palpable historic change in the way businesses and workers create value, our nation needs to address the associated dislocations that emerge, especially among workers who see the security of their jobs and their lives threatened. Societies cannot thrive when significant segments perceive its functioning as unjust."

—"TECHNOLOGY AND THE ECONOMY"; BEFORE THE ECONOMIC CLUB OF
NEW YORK, NEW YORK CITY; JANUARY 13, 2000

"To be sure, we, as a society, shall continue for some time to face difficult questions about how to ensure that all segments of our society are afforded opportunities to participate in the greater prosperity. But the improvements in the economic climate that seem to be in train should provide the macro stability and micro incentives needed to foster the investments in human capital that will help redress the imbalances that have concerned all of us in recent years."

—BEFORE THE CONCORD COALITION, NEW YORK CITY; NOVEMBER 2, 1995

• • •

When considering differences in class wealth and well-being, the temptation is to look at the traditional measure of income. Greenspan takes a different approach, looking at consumption to help quantify the issue.

"Despite our best efforts to measure trends in income and wealth, I believe that even those measures—by themselves—cannot yield a complete answer to the question of trends in material or economic well-being. In the United States, we observe a noticeable difference between trends in the dispersion of holdings of *claims* to goods and services—that is, income and wealth—and trends in the dispersion of actual consumption, the bottom-line determinant of material well-being. Ultimately, we are interested in whether households have the means to meet their needs for goods and for services, including those such as education and medical care, that build and maintain human capital."

—"INCOME INEQUALITY: ISSUES AND POLICY OPTIONS";
AT A SYMPOSIUM SPONSORED BY THE FEDERAL RESERVE BANK OF
KANSAS CITY, JACKSON HOLE, WYOMING; AUGUST 28, 1998

• • •

A society cannot begin to tackle economic disparity until inflation is under control.

"We must pursue monetary conditions in which stable prices contribute to maximizing sustainable long-run growth. Such disciplined policies will offer the best underpinnings for identifying opportunities to channel growing knowledge, innovation, and capital investment into the creation of wealth that, in turn, will lift living standards as broadly as possible. Moreover, as evidenced by this symposium, sustaining a healthy economy and a stable financial system naturally permits us to take the time to focus efforts on addressing the distributional issues facing our society and on other challenging issues that may remain out in the cold."

—"INCOME INEQUALITY: ISSUES AND POLICY OPTIONS";
AT A SYMPOSIUM SPONSORED BY THE FEDERAL RESERVE BANK OF
KANSAS CITY, JACKSON HOLE, WYOMING; AUGUST 28, 1998

• • •

Although public subsidies may be good short-term fixes, they are detrimental in the long run because communities become dependent on them.

"Heavy community development dependence on public subsidies, while possibly beneficial in the short term, can engender project defaults and displacements, should that stream disappear. Public subsidies are subject to political and budgetary whims and forces. Sustainable community development should not be hostage to unreliable long-term financing. The challenge to the industry is to find alternate methods of packaging safe and sound community development deals, which do not depend on the continued existence of significant quantities of public money."

—"ECONOMIC DEVELOPMENT IN LOW- AND MODERATE-INCOME
COMMUNITIES"; AT A COMMUNITY FORUM ON COMMUNITY REINVESTMENT
AND ACCESS TO CREDIT: CALIFORNIA'S CHALLENGE,
LOS ANGELES; JANUARY 12, 1998

• • •

If markets were perfect, there would be no discrimination.

"If markets were fully efficient—that is, if all resources were allocated optimally and fully employed without discrimination—profit maximizers would arbitrage away such noneconomic differences (as race) in the returns to human capital and other productive resources."

—"THE UNDEREMPLOYMENT OF MINORITIES";
AT THE WALL STREET PROJECT ANNIVERSARY CONFERENCE OF THE
RAINBOW/PUSH COALITION, NEW YORK CITY; JANUARY 16, 1998

• • •

Greenspan is brutally honest when he says that there's little that can done to fix child poverty immediately. The only cure is to increase the skills of parents.

"On the issue of child poverty, clearly there's nothing that can change that right now. The child can't move out into the workforce and create a dot.com company and elevate himself out of poverty. It's a process in which the parents and skill creation of various generations has got to be moved up. While broad training is useful, it is in no way anywhere close to on-the-job training as far as the capacity to bring up skills is concerned. One of the key important aspects of the extraordinary economy we now experience is the large number of people that moved out of welfare, off unemployment roles and into jobs, and for the first time have had a sense of self-confidence in working that they had not previously had and probably created new lives for vast, vast numbers of people. The degree to which we can substitute on-the-job training—getting people at the lower ends of the ladder—the quicker we can do that, the more broadly we can do that, the better off we'll be. We've already seen a significant decline in the unemployment rate of those with less than high school education. This means that what we're doing is taking people by definition substantially unskilled and giving them the chance to create those skills.

"I cannot say that I necessarily feel that it's going to be easy to confront the types of problems that you raise, because the major issues that I see the United States has during this affluent period is the question of distribution of income. No society succeeds unless virtually all of its participants believe that it's fair and gives people opportunities. It's very important for us to focus on this as we view this extraordinary technology, this huge increase in productivity and standards of living, and recognize that it is important for the functioning of the system that we make sure that all participate in that."

—BEFORE THE SENATE BANKING COMMITTEE; JANUARY 26, 2000

# Greenspan on:
# Globalization

One of Greenspan's hot buttons is the intertwining economies among countries. In his presentations, he hammers home the idea that no country operates in a vacuum. Although not all national crises are contagious immediately, they do eventually spread globally. As chairman of the Fed, Greenspan is part of the coterie of central bankers who work through the International Monetary Fund (IMF) to help settle economic issues that cross national borders. Many times he finds himself in the politically sensitive position of offering suggestions to countries on how to handle their economic affairs. Most often, he gives advice through his public speeches.

"It is just not credible that the United States can remain an oasis of prosperity unaffected by a world that is experiencing greatly increased stress."
—AT THE HAAS ANNUAL BUSINESS FACULTY RESEARCH DIALOGUE, UNIVERSITY OF CALIFORNIA, BERKELEY; SEPTEMBER 4, 1998

"The globalization of capital markets offers many benefits in terms of increased competition, reduced costs of financial intermediation that benefit both savers and borrowers, more efficient allocation of capital, and the more rapid spread of innovations. However, this internationalization does pose certain risks as well: The United States has become more vulnerable to disturbances originating outside its borders. The Federal Reserve has been actively interested in efforts to limit risks in international payments and settlement systems. In cooperation with authorities in other countries, the Federal Reserve has pressed for improved capital adequacy for banks and other financial intermediaries."

—BEFORE THE COMMITTEE ON WAYS AND MEANS,
U.S. HOUSE OF REPRESENTATIVES; JANUARY 25, 1990

• • •

Over the years, many in Congress have called for the United States to drop its support of the IMF. Greenspan disagrees, believing that the IMF is a vital resource.

"Convincing a sovereign nation to alter destructive policies that impair its own performance and threaten contagion to its neighbors is best handled by an international financial institution, such as the IMF. What we have in place today to respond to crises should be supported even as we work to improve those mechanisms and institutions."

—"THE CURRENT ASIA CRISIS AND THE DYNAMICS OF INTERNATIONAL
FINANCE"; BEFORE THE COMMITTEE ON BANKING AND FINANCIAL SERVICES,
U.S. HOUSE OF REPRESENTATIVES; JANUARY 30, 1998

"The IMF really requires a fundamental review in all its aspects, but not now. It's as if you want to get to work in the morning and all you have is a bicycle, but you want to go by limousine. The IMF may be a bicycle, but it's all we have."

—"INTERNATIONAL ECONOMIC AND FINANCIAL SYSTEM";
BEFORE THE COMMITTEE ON BANKING AND FINANCIAL SERVICES, U.S.
HOUSE OF REPRESENTATIVES; SEPTEMBER 16, 1998

• • •

Greenspan warns of the dangers of short-term interbank funding.

"Despite its importance for distributing savings to their most valued use, short-term interbank funding, especially cross border, may turn out to be the Achilles' heel of an international financial system that is subject to wide variations in financial confidence. This phenomenon, which is all too common in our domestic experience, may be particularly dangerous in an international setting."

—"THE CURRENT ASIA CRISIS AND THE DYNAMICS OF INTERNATIONAL FINANCE"; BEFORE THE COMMITTEE ON BANKING AND FINANCIAL SERVICES, U.S. HOUSE OF REPRESENTATIVES; JANUARY 30, 1998

• • •

Because a national crisis can become an international crisis, government regulators should never abrogate their responsibility for supervision.

"In this rapidly expanding international financial system, the primary protection from adverse financial disturbances is effective counterparty surveillance and, hence, government regulation and supervision should seek to produce an environment in which counterparties can most effectively oversee the credit risks of potential transactions."

—"THE CURRENT ASIA CRISIS AND THE DYNAMICS OF INTERNATIONAL FINANCE"; BEFORE THE COMMITTEE ON BANKING AND FINANCIAL SERVICES, U.S. HOUSE OF REPRESENTATIVES; JANUARY 30, 1998

• • •

Greenspan noted that investors lost more than $700 billion in Asian stocks; U.S. investors about $30 billion of that.

"Events in Asia reinforce once more the fact that, while our burgeoning global system is efficient and makes a substantial contribution to standards of living worldwide, that same efficiency exposes and punishes underlying economic imprudence swiftly and decisively. Regrettably, the very efficiency that contributes so much to our global system also facilitates the transmission of financial disturbances far more effectively than ever before."

—"IMPLICATIONS OF RECENT ASIAN DEVELOPMENTS FOR COMMUNITY BANKING"; BEFORE THE ANNUAL CONVENTION OF THE INDEPENDENT BANKERS ASSOCIATION OF AMERICA, HONOLULU; MARCH 3, 1998

• • •

We don't fully understand how global markets operate. Unless we do, Greenspan warns, we may be unable to stem worldwide financial crises from spreading.

"Global financial markets, engendered by the rapid proliferation of cross-border financial flows and products, have developed a capability of transmitting mistakes at a far faster pace throughout the financial system in ways that were unknown a generation ago. Today's international financial system is sufficiently different, in so many respects, from its predecessors that it can reasonably be characterized as new, as distinct from being merely a continuing evolution from the past. As a consequence, it is urgent that we accelerate our efforts to develop a sophisticated understanding of how this high-tech financial system works. Specifically, we need such an understanding if we are to minimize the chances that we will experience a systemic disruption beyond our degree of comprehension or our ability to respond effectively."

—"UNDERSTANDING TODAY'S INTERNATIONAL FINANCIAL SYSTEM"; BEFORE THE 34TH ANNUAL CONFERENCE ON BANK STRUCTURE AND COMPETITION OF THE FEDERAL RESERVE BANK OF CHICAGO, CHICAGO; MAY 7, 1998

"This burgeoning global telecommunications system has been demonstrated to be a highly efficient structure that has significantly facilitated cross-border trade in goods and services and, accordingly, has made a substantial contribution to standards of living worldwide. Its efficiency exposes and punishes underlying economic weakness swiftly and decisively. Regrettably, it also appears to have facilitated the transmission of financial disturbances far more effectively than ever before. The crisis in Mexico several years ago was the first such episode associated with our new high-tech international financial system. The current Asian crisis is the second.

"We do not as yet fully understand the new system's dynamics. We are learning fast, and need to update and modify our institutions and practices to reduce the risks inherent in the new regime."

—"RISK MANAGEMENT IN THE GLOBAL FINANCIAL SYSTEM"; BEFORE THE ANNUAL FINANCIAL MARKETS CONFERENCE OF THE FEDERAL RESERVE BANK OF ATLANTA, MIAMI BEACH, FLORIDA; FEBRUARY 27, 1998

• • •

One downside of globalization is the rapid spread of investor fear.

"With the new more sophisticated financial markets punishing errant government policy behavior far more expeditiously than in the past, vicious cycles are evidently emerging more often. Once they are triggered, damage control is difficult. Once the web of confidence, which supports the financial system, is breached, it is difficult to restore quickly. The loss of confidence can trigger rapid and disruptive changes in the patterns of finance, which, in turn, feeds back on exchange rates and asset prices. Moreover, investor concerns that weaknesses revealed in one economy may be present in others that are similarly situated means that the loss of confidence can quickly spread to other countries."

—"IMPLICATIONS OF RECENT ASIAN DEVELOPMENTS FOR COMMUNITY BANKING"; BEFORE THE ANNUAL CONVENTION OF THE INDEPENDENT BANKERS ASSOCIATION OF AMERICA, HONOLULU; MARCH 3, 1998

• • •

The crisis in Mexico was the first wake-up call that national economic turmoil can spread.

"Although the speed of transmission of positive economic events has been an important plus for the world in recent years, it is becoming increasingly obvious—and Mexico is the first major case—that significant mistakes in macroeconomic policy also reverberate around the world at a prodigious pace. In any event, progress—and indeed developments affecting the emerging global financial system are truly that—is not reversible. We must learn to live with it."
—BEFORE THE COMMITTEE ON FOREIGN RELATIONS, U.S. SENATE;
JANUARY 26, 1995

• • •

Two years later, Greenspan reiterates the idea that global contagion is now a fact of life.

"While the speed of transmission of positive economic events has been an important plus for the world economy in recent years, it is becoming increasingly obvious, as evidenced by recent events in Thailand and its neighbors and several years ago in Mexico, that significant macroeconomic policy mistakes also reverberate around the world at a prodigious pace. In any event, technological progress is not reversible. We must learn to live with it."
—AT THE 15TH ANNUAL MONETARY CONFERENCE OF THE CATO INSTITUTE,
WASHINGTON, D.C.; OCTOBER 14, 1997

"The turmoil in the European Exchange Rate mechanism in 1992, the plunge in the exchange value of the Mexican peso at the end of 1994 and early 1995, and the recent sharp exchange rate adjustments in a number of Asian economies have shown how the new world of financial trading can punish policy misalignments, actual or perceived, with amazing alacrity. This is new. Even as recently as fifteen or twenty years ago, the size of the international financial system was a fraction of what it is today. Contagion effects were more limited, and, thus, breakdowns carried fewer negative consequences."

—AT THE 15TH ANNUAL MONETARY CONFERENCE OF THE CATO INSTITUTE, WASHINGTON, D.C.; OCTOBER 14, 1997

• • •

Countries must update their financial infrastructure to compete in the global marketplace.

"When domestic financial systems fail for lack of adequate institutional infrastructures, the solution is not to turn back to a less turbulent, but also less prosperous, past regime of capital controls, but to strengthen the domestic institutions that are the prerequisite for engaging in today's international financial system."

—"INTERNATIONAL ECONOMIC AND FINANCIAL SYSTEM"; BEFORE THE COMMITTEE ON BANKING AND FINANCIAL SERVICES, U.S. HOUSE OF REPRESENTATIVES; SEPTEMBER 16, 1998

• • •

Stable governments have stable currencies.

"At the end of the day the issue is not the stability of currencies, but the underlying policies that engender stable currencies. Open economies, governed by a rule of law with sound monetary, trade and fiscal policies, rarely experience exchange rate problems that destabilize those economies to the degree we have seen in Asia."

—BROADCAST TO THE ANNUAL MEETING OF THE SECURITIES INDUSTRY ASSOCIATION IN BOCA RATON, FLORIDA; NOVEMBER 6, 1998

"We have observed that global financial markets, as currently organized, do not always achieve an appropriate equilibrium, or at least require time to stabilize."

—"The Current Asian Crisis"; before the Subcommittee on Foreign Operations of the Committee on Appropriations, U.S. Senate; March 3, 1998

• • •

Central bankers must appreciate that their actions don't stop at their country's borders.

"Monetary policy in all countries must take account of its effects on, and feedback from, the rest of the world. Many financial services provided by central banks involve cross-border transactions of one kind or another. These international relationships add still one more degree of complexity to the already complex lives of central bankers. That is one of our challenges."

—at the Catholic University Leuven, Leuven, Belgium; January 14, 1997

"While there are many policy considerations that arise as a consequence of the rapidly expanding global financial system, the most important is the necessity of maintaining stability in the prices of goods and services and confidence in domestic financial markets. Failure to do so is apt to exact far greater consequences as a result of cross-border capital movements than might have prevailed a generation ago."

—"Humphrey-Hawkins, Monetary Policy Testimony and Report to the Congress"; February 22, 1995

• • •

Recognizing and planning for risk may be a country's best defense against international economic instability.

"We cannot turn back the clock on technology—and we should not try to do so. Rather, we should recognize that, if it is technology that has imparted the current stress to markets, technology can be employed to contain it. Enhancements to financial institutions' internal risk-management systems arguably constitute the most effective countermeasure to the increased potential instability of the global financial system. Improving the efficiency of the world's payment systems is clearly another."

—AT THE 15TH ANNUAL MONETARY CONFERENCE OF THE CATO INSTITUTE,
WASHINGTON, D.C.; OCTOBER 14, 1997

• • •

Just as Greenspan calls for the judicious use of a safety net for domestic banks, because it could cause them to become reckless in their actions, so too he calls for the same restraint in the international arena.

"In providing any international financial assistance, we need to be mindful of the desirability of minimizing the impression that international authorities stand ready to guarantee the liabilities of failed domestic businesses. To do otherwise could lead to distorted investments and could ultimately unbalance the world financial system."

—BEFORE THE JOINT ECONOMIC COMMITTEE,
U.S. CONGRESS; OCTOBER 29, 1997

• • •

Referring to the crisis in Asia:

"We used to describe capital flight as hot money. But we soon recognized that it was not the money that was hot, but the place it was running from."

—AT THE ECONOMIC CLUB OF NEW YORK,
NEW YORK CITY; DECEMBER 2, 1997

• • •

Central banks with different ideologies can coexist as long as they agree to common standards of behavior.

"So long as we adhere in principle to a common prudential standard, it is appropriate that differing regulatory regimes may exist side by side at any point in time, responding to differing conditions between banking systems or across individual banks within a single system. Perhaps the appropriate analogy is to computer-chip manufacturers. Even as the next generation of chip is being planned, two or three generations of chip—for example, Pentium IIs, Pentium Pros, and Pentium MMXs—are being marketed, and at the same time, older generations of chip continue to perform yeoman duty within specific applications. Given evolving financial markets, the question is not whether the Basle standard will be changed but how and why each new round of change will occur and to which market segment it will apply."
—"The Role of Capital in Optimal Banking Supervision and Regulation"; *Federal Reserve Bank of New York Economic Policy Review;* October 1998

"Banking systems are the product of their underlying cultures and the business relationships these cultures have developed. At present I see no evidence to suggest that one type of structure is inherently better than another. Therefore, I see no compelling need to seek a one-size-fits-all resolution to the issue of ownership interlocks for competitive equity. Rather, each country can experiment with its own system based on its own unique circumstances, concerns, and historic legacy."
—"International Financial Integration"; before the Federation of Bankers Associations of Japan, Tokyo; October 14, 1992

• • •

After the fall of the Soviet Union, Greenspan commented on why its system failed.

"Central planning of the type that prevailed in postwar Eastern Europe and the Soviet Union represented one attempt to fashion an economic system that eliminated this competitive churning and its presumed wastefulness. But when that system eliminated the risk of failure, it also stifled the incentive to innovate and to prosper. Central planning fostered stasis: In many respects, the eastern bloc economies marched in place for more than four decades."

—BEFORE THE SUBCOMMITTEE ON ECONOMIC GROWTH AND CREDIT FORMATION OF THE COMMITTEE ON BANKING, FINANCE, AND URBAN AFFAIRS, U.S. HOUSE OF REPRESENTATIVES; JULY 20, 1993

• • •

Because of telecommunications, consumers learn what is available outside their nation's borders. This demand breaks down isolation and forces change.

"New telecommunications technologies made it very difficult for the autarchic societies of the former Soviet Union to sustain their isolation in the face of the growing relative affluence of the West. News could no longer be bottled up. Even in the West, the stultification of protectionism became increasingly evident as new consumer products entered the world markets *en masse*. The political pressures to deregulate moribund industries and open up borders to trade soon became irresistible."

—BEFORE THE DALLAS AMBASSADORS FORUM, DALLAS, TEXAS; APRIL 16, 1999

• • •

Greenspan was asked by Sen. Alfonse D'Amato (R–New York) whether he was concerned about growing foreign investment in the United States, particularly by Japanese companies that were buying real estate in New York City and elsewhere. "Japan is buying America and leasing it back to us," suggested D'Amato.

"On the contrary, the integration of the world economies . . . is inevitable . . . and is a desirable trend," answered Greenspan, who pointed out that foreign-owned businesses find it in their best interests to become good corporate citizens.

• • •

"We will find that foreign investment in the United States will be a plus."
—BEFORE THE HOUSE-SENATE JOINT ECONOMIC COMMITTEE;
MARCH 15, 1988

• • •

Several years later, Greenspan reiterated the benefits to the U.S. economy of foreign investments.

"Concern about foreign investment in the United States tends to focus on direct investment; highly visible purchases, such as Rockefeller Center, Columbia Pictures, and Bloomingdale's, have given rise to fears about the selling of America at bargain basement prices. However, little attention is paid to the benefits of direct investment. The operations of multinational companies play an important role in facilitating the growth of world trade in goods, services, and information. Trade and direct investment are intimately related; transactions between direct investment affiliates and their U.S. or foreign parents accounted for 35 percent of U.S. merchandise exports and 40 percent of U.S. imports in 1987—the latest year for which data are available. It is essentially impossible to separate trade from investment and vice versa. Foreign investment in the United States spurs competition, provides infusions of new capital and technology into industries like steel, and speeds the spread of technological advances."

—BEFORE THE COMMITTEE ON WAYS AND MEANS, U.S. HOUSE OF REPRESENTATIVES; JANUARY 25, 1990

"Acquisitions of U.S. companies by foreigners present somewhat different issues. The analysis of mergers and acquisitions in general is controversial, but one conclusion with which nearly all investigators would concur is that the American stockholders of takeover targets are big gainers. The former owners of acquired U.S. companies can reinvest these funds in other enterprises that they judge to have the highest returns. As for foreigners who outbid U.S. competitors for U.S. companies, recent news indicates that overly optimistic estimates of future earnings may have been an important factor in several important cases."

—BEFORE THE COMMITTEE ON WAYS AND MEANS, U.S. HOUSE OF REPRESENTATIVES; JANUARY 25, 1990

# Greenspan on:
# Gold

reenspan's beliefs have been remarkably constant over the years; however, his comments on gold and its role in the economy reveal a change of heart. Although never a staunch gold bug, he did nonetheless, as a young man, show his interest in gold as a stabilizing force and a backer of currency. Years later, he admitted that a gold standard can be constrictive in a free and fast-moving global market.

"Gold was such an anchor or rule, prior to World War I, but it was first compromised and eventually abandoned because it restrained the type of discretionary monetary and fiscal policies that modern democracies appear to value."

—AT THE 15TH ANNIVERSARY CONFERENCE OF THE CENTER FOR ECONOMIC POLICY RESEARCH AT STANFORD UNIVERSITY, STANFORD, CALIFORNIA; SEPTEMBER 5, 1997

• • •

The following is one of Greenspan's earliest published writings. Written during a time when he was involved with the teachings of Ayn Rand, the piece, excerpted here, discusses how gold can play a role in preventing governments from over-spending if their currency is pegged to the precious metal. Overspending leads to inflation, and therefore gold can help stop inflation. This argument, while compelling, is too simplistic. Remember, he was young man when he wrote this.

"Under a gold standard, the amount of credit that an economy can support is determined by the economy's tangible assets, since every credit instrument is ultimately a claim on some tangible asset. But government bonds are not backed by tangible wealth, only by the government's promise to pay out of future tax revenues, and cannot easily be absorbed by the financial markets. A large volume of new government bonds can be sold to the public only at progressively higher interest rates. Thus, government deficit spending under a gold standard is severely limited.

"The abandonment of the gold standard made it possible for the welfare statists to use the banking system as a means to an unlimited expansion of credit. They have created paper reserves in the form of government bonds which—through a complex series of steps—the banks accept in place of tangible assets and treat as if they were an actual deposit, i.e., as the equivalent of what was formerly a deposit of gold. The holder of a government bond or of a bank deposit created by paper reserves believes that he has a valid claim on a real asset. But the fact is that there are now more claims outstanding than real assets.

". . . In the absence of the gold standard, there is no way to protect savings from confiscation through inflation. There is no safe store of value. If there were, the government would have to make its holding illegal, as was done in the case of gold. If everyone decided, for example, to convert all his bank deposits to silver or copper or any other good, and thereafter declined to accept checks as payment for goods, bank deposits would lose their purchasing power and government-created bank credit would be worthless as a claim on goods.

The financial policy of the welfare state requires that there be no way for the owners of wealth to protect themselves.

"This is the shabby secret of the welfare statists' tirades against gold. Deficit spending is simply a scheme for the 'hidden' confiscation of wealth. Gold stands in the way of this insidious process. It stands as a protector of property rights. If one grasps this, one has no difficulty in understanding the statists' antagonism toward the gold standard."

—"GOLD AND ECONOMIC FREEDOM," *THE OBJECTIVIST* NEWSLETTER, 1966. (THE ARTICLE WAS REPRINTED IN THE BOOK *CAPITALISM, THE UNKNOWN IDEAL* BY AYN RAND WITH ADDITIONAL ARTICLES BY ALAN GREENSPAN AND ROBERT HESSEN, SIGNET BOOKS, 1967.)

• • •

About 20 years later, before Congress, Greenspan discusses the gold standard, which was abandoned in the early 1970s. Gold used to be considered an excellent indicator of inflation because investors would buy gold as a hedge against rising prices. Greenspan notes that although it is somewhat useful as an economic indicator its forecasting value is limited.

"Gold is relevant and useful as an indicator of a flight from currency. However, we must be careful not to interpret every change in the price of gold as meaning that."

• • •

As for returning to the gold standard, he notes that the dollar has taken over as the currency of choice worldwide.

"There are too many practical problems associated with restoration of a gold standard, not the least of which is the huge block of outstanding dollar claims in world financial markets today to make this a useful avenue of development."

—BEFORE A JOINT HEARING OF TWO HOUSE BANKING SUBCOMMITTEES; DECEMBER 18, 1987

# Greenspan on:

# Housing

**D**espite galactic rises in the stock market over the past 10 years, Greenspan makes the case that home sales and not stock gains is the largest single contribution to what's been called the "wealth effect"—a sense of financial well-being that spurs consumer spending.

He says that sales of existing homes account for about a sixth of wealth-effect spending and its effects are likely to increase in coming years. Consumers consider homes a permanent investment as opposed to stock ownership, which is considered transitory.

---

For more consumers to enjoy the wealth effect, it's vital for them to own homes.

"While home prices do on occasion decline, large declines are rare; the general experience of homeowners is a modest, but persistent rise in home values that is perceived to be largely permanent. This experience contrasts markedly from volatile and often-ephemeral gains in stock market wealth. . . . Lowering the costs of home ownership is particularly important for increasing homeownership rates among young adults."

—AT A MORTGAGE CONFERENCE SPONSORED BY AMERICA'S COMMUNITY BANKERS, WASHINGTON, D.C.; NOVEMBER 2, 1999

• • •

Mortgage lenders have chided Greenspan for raising interest rates, which they claim deters home purchases, and want him to lower rates instead. Greenspan counters that lowering rates can be just as detrimental to home sales as raising interest rates because it gives an impression of price instability, which makes people wary of buying anything—including houses.

"A central message of the past couple of decades is that, if the real estate industry is to prosper consistently, you need stability, be it in the availability and cost of credit or in consumer confidence and demand. History is replete with examples of a general principle, namely that excesses lead to problems. Boom-and-bust cycles are no friend of real estate professionals or your customers. For one thing, these cycles have often involved sharply rising house prices followed by plummeting values. Home price volatility leads to unrealistic price expectations, which can play havoc with your business and make it more difficult for your customers to adjust their housing as their personal circumstances change. To make a major purchase, most consumers need to feel that the future will be at least as favorable as the present. They need to feel comfortable that they will have the income to make their monthly mortgage payments. And they must feel secure that their investment is safe—that is, that house prices won't collapse."

—BEFORE THE BOARD OF DIRECTORS, NATIONAL ASSOCIATION OF REALTORS, WASHINGTON, D.C.; MAY 16, 1995

• • •

Greenspan believes that consumers feel more confident with stability than almost any other condition. When these comments were made, the average rate for a 30-year, fixed-rate mortgage was 9.13 percent, a sharp increase from 7 percent a year earlier.

"Some have criticized these rate hikes. But I am convinced that if we had not acted, your business would have suffered . . . Confident consumers at 9 percent mortgage rates are better customers than nervous consumers at 7 percent rates.

". . . Consumers are not willing to buy a house unless they are confident they will retain their jobs and that the value of the home will not decline . . ."

—BEFORE THE NATIONAL ASSOCIATION OF HOME BUILDERS IN HOUSTON; JANUARY 28, 1995

"It is hard to overestimate the importance of house price trends on consumer psyches and behavior. Even with all the financial innovations and new forms of investment open to individuals, houses remain the single most important store of wealth for much of the population. To put the estimated $4 trillion in home equity in perspective, it averages out to about $65,000 per homeowner.

"Consumers view their home equity as a cushion or security blanket against the possibility of future hard times. But many consumers also tap their home equity directly, for a variety of purposes, including home improvements, auto purchases, college tuition, and debt consolidation."

—BEFORE THE BOARD OF DIRECTORS, NATIONAL ASSOCIATION OF REALTORS, WASHINGTON, D.C.; MAY 16, 1995

# Greenspan on:
# Humor

Because of his position and power, Alan Greenspan must be careful what he says in public—even in jest. So it's not often that he tells a joke or makes a humorous comment lest it be taken seriously by Greenspan watchers. Nevertheless, his dry wit emerges every once in a while.

---

"I do not perceive the end of the shopping mall, if for no other reason than I have been strongly advised that shopping is not solely an economic phenomenon."
—BEFORE THE BUSINESS COUNCIL, COMPOSED OF CHIEF EXECUTIVES OF THE NATION'S TOP COMPANIES, BOCA RATON; OCTOBER 28, 1999

• • •

Even in small talk, Greenspan chats in a convoluted manner. Although he almost never speaks to reporters, Greenspan, just before a Senate testimony, said a few words about the baseball home-run race between Chicago Cubs outfielder Sammy Sosa and St. Louis Cardinals first baseman Mark McGwire. Sosa was quoted as saying that McGwire "will finish a little bit higher" in the race to set a season home-run record. Sosa had been on a bad streak, coming up empty for twenty-one at-bats.

Jibed Greenspan, "I seriously question whether Sammy Sosa is correct in conceding he will not win."

Ninety minutes after Greenspan's remark, Sosa hit his 64th and 65th homers, pulling even with McGwire.

—INFORMAL REMARKS TO REPORTERS,
WASHINGTON, D.C.; SEPTEMBER 23, 1998

•  •  •

In an exchange with Sen. Judd Gregg (R–New Hampshire), Greenspan made a little fun of himself.

GREGG: Mr. Chairman, you talked about the need for an ad hoc remedy at this time because you can't put in place the long-term actions which would require—which are required to get what you think is a sound financial process throughout the world. Would part of that ad hoc remedy or an element of that ad hoc remedy be constructively impacted by a rate cut in the United States?

GREENSPAN: I thought that would be the second or third question.

GREGG: Let's get it out early, you know.

GREENSPAN: Obviously, I can't be directly responsive to that question. All I can say to you—

GREGG: I'm talking about in theoretical terms, in the ad hoc—in the ad hoc remedy concept.

GREENSPAN: I got the point. I've been able to string more words into fewer ideas than anybody I know, and I'm continuing to do that.

—BEFORE THE COMMITTEE ON THE BUDGET, U.S. SENATE;
SEPTEMBER 23, 1998

•  •  •

Asked what effect the news of their engagement might have on Wall Street, his fiancée Andrea Mitchell replied, "I hope they will not become irrationally exuberant."

—"MERGERS AND ACQUISITIONS; FED'S ALAN GREENSPAN TO WED NBC'S
ANDREA MITCHELL," *THE WASHINGTON POST,* DECEMBER 31, 1996

• • •

The following story, reported by newspapers and wire services, illustrates Greenspan's understanding of the power of language. It's a pretty good joke, too.

Alan Greenspan and Arthur Levitt, chairman of the Securities and Exchange Commission, were playing golf early one morning at the Chevy Chase Club. Greenspan told this joke: Three patients at a mental institution wanted to be released. The head psychiatrist gave them a simple test: What is two plus two? The first patient said, "Five." The second said, "Wednesday." The third got it right. "Four," he said. The first two patients returned to their ward. Patient three was free to go.

"By the way," asked the doctor as the man was leaving, "how did you know the answer?"

"Easy," said the patient. "I just added five plus Wednesday."

• • •

"I am quite pleased and gratified to receive the Adam Smith Award this evening. Having been a bank regulator for ten years, I need something to remind me that the world operates just fine with a minimum of us."

—AT THE ANNUAL CONFERENCE OF THE ASSOCIATION OF PRIVATE ENTERPRISE EDUCATION, ARLINGTON, VIRGINIA; APRIL 12, 1997

• • •

Greenspan has been criticized for what's called "Fedspeak," a mixture of obfuscation and even more obfuscation. Once, in 1997, he told a Congressman: "I know you believe you understand what you think I said. But I am not sure you realize that what you heard is not what I meant."

In late February 1997, Sen. Robert Bennett (R–Utah) told Greenspan: "Either you're getting clearer, or I'm finally beginning to break the code."

• • •

Here, Greenspan is referring to his "irrational exuberance" comment that rocked the markets.

"It is always with mixed feelings of pleasure and trepidation that I accept an invitation to speak at the American Bankers Association annual convention. I still have a disconcerted remembrance of my acceptance of your first invitation, which had been scheduled for October 20, 1987. That speech had to be scratched at the last minute as the result of a certain adversity in stock price adjustments the day before. Experience suggests, however, that history does not repeat with a fixed periodicity and, besides, I have crossed my fingers."
—AT THE ANNUAL CONVENTION OF THE AMERICAN BANKERS ASSOCIATION, BOSTON; OCTOBER 5, 1997

"I can assure you that it is not a goal of monetary policy to encourage fluctuations in interest rates, even if it does make your lives more interesting."
—BEFORE THE BOARD OF DIRECTORS, NATIONAL ASSOCIATION OF REALTORS, WASHINGTON, D.C.; MAY 16, 1995

"If I say something which you understand fully in this regard, I probably made a mistake."
—BEFORE THE SENATE BANKING COMMITTEE; JUNE 20, 1995

"I must tell you that if I read some of the reports in the newspapers about all the things that are going on, remember, good news is really on page thirty-five while bad news is right smack up front. For those of you who want to get an objective view of what is going on in the world, it's probably wise to put your newspapers in your In Box and leave them there for about a week, and then you can read them. You'll probably get a more objective view of what is going on."

—BEFORE THE 40TH ANNUAL MEETING OF THE NATIONAL ASSOCIATION FOR BUSINESS ECONOMICS (NABE), WASHINGTON, D.C., OCTOBER 3–7, 1998

Q. If we don't get a budget resolution, isn't whoever is the Fed chairman going to have to keep a pretty tight hold on the money supply?

A. His job will be difficult. Fed policy is often hostage to fiscal policy.

Q. If the President decides not to reappoint Chairman Volcker, do you think it would be wise for him to appoint a well-known monetarist?

A. I would just as soon not characterize what the President should or should not do on this issue. It's easy for us to stand on the sidelines and make suggestions, but he has some difficult decisions. I suspect he'll do fine by himself.

Q. You have been mentioned as a possible successor to Mr. Volcker as chairman of the Federal Reserve Board. If the job is offered to you, would you consider it?

A. I would merely repeat the answer to the question immediately preceding.

—"THE LONG-TERM BOOM NOW IN PROSPECT," INTERVIEW WITH ALAN GREENSPAN, LEADING ECONOMIST; *U.S. NEWS & WORLD REPORT*, JUNE 6, 1983

• • •

After he was sworn in by President Reagan, Greenspan offered this ironic comment about the challenges ahead.

"Perhaps I should thank in advance the creators of all those events that will make the next four years easygoing— inflation which always stays put, a stock market which is always a bull, a dollar which is always stable, interest rates which stay low and employment which stays high. But most assuredly, I would be thankful to those who have the capability of repealing the laws of arithmetic which would make all of the foregoing possible."

—AT GREENSPAN'S SWEARING-IN CEREMONY; AUGUST 11, 1987

"I find misplaced the fear that the deficit reduction can be overdone and create a degree of 'fiscal drag' that would significantly harm the economy. In our current political environment, to presume that the Congress and the President would jointly cut too much from the deficit too soon is in the words of my predecessor 'nothing I would lose sleep over.'"

—BEFORE THE COMMITTEE ON BANKING, HOUSING, AND URBAN AFFAIRS, U.S. SENATE; FEBRUARY 19, 1993

# Greenspan on:
# Inflation

---

**C**all it price stability or call it inflation, Greenspan has set his sights on taming it. Like the previous chairman, Paul Volcker, Greenspan believes that price stability is the key to economic prosperity and he has marshaled all of the forces of monetary policy to keeping inflation low and stable. His goal has never been zero inflation, but he has attempted to keep it at levels low enough that consumers and companies don't have to factor it in when deciding how to invest their capital.

---

"I believe firmly that a key ingredient in achieving the highest possible levels of productivity, real incomes, and living standards is the achievement of price stability."
—BEFORE THE COMMITTEE ON FINANCE, U.S. SENATE; JANUARY 25, 1995

"This greater ability to pare costs, increase production flexibility, and expand capacity is arguably the major reason why inflationary pressures have been held in check in recent years."
—BEFORE THE HOUSE BANKING COMMITTEE; JULY 22, 1999

• • •

Greenspan sees the tightening labor market as an inflation trigger.

"There can be little doubt that, if the pool of job seekers shrinks sufficiently, upward pressures on wage costs are inevitable. Such cost increases have invariably presaged rising inflation in the past, and presumably would in the future, which would threaten the economic expansion."

—BEFORE THE HOUSE BANKING COMMITTEE; JULY 22, 1999

• • •

Could there be a psychological component to inflation? Greenspan believes so.

"The economy has become less inflation-prone than in the past, so that the chances of an inflationary breakout arguably are, at least for now, less than they would have been under similar conditions in earlier cycles."

—"THE FEDERAL RESERVE'S SEMIANNUAL REPORT ON MONETARY POLICY"; BEFORE THE COMMITTEE ON BANKING, HOUSING, AND URBAN AFFAIRS, U.S. SENATE; FEBRUARY 23, 1999

"The role of expectations in the inflation process is crucial. Even expectations not validated by economic fundamentals can themselves add appreciably to wage and price pressures for a considerable period, potentially derailing the economy from its growth track.

"Why, for example, despite an above-normal rate of unemployment and permanent layoffs, have uncertainties about job security not led to further moderation in wage increases? The answer appears to lie, at least in part, in the deep-seated anticipations understandably harbored by workers that inflation is likely to reaccelerate in the near term and undercut their real wages."

—BEFORE THE SUBCOMMITTEE ON ECONOMIC GROWTH AND CREDIT FORMATION OF THE COMMITTEE ON BANKING, FINANCE, AND URBAN AFFAIRS, U.S. HOUSE OF REPRESENTATIVES; JULY 20, 1993

"Simply put, while the pursuit of price stability does not rule out misfortune, it lowers its probability. If firms are convinced that the general price level will remain stable, they will reserve increases in their sales prices of goods and services as a last resort, for fear that such increases could mean loss of market share. Similarly, if households are convinced of price stability, they will not see variations in relative prices as reasons to change their long-run inflation expectations. Thus, continuing to make progress toward this legislated objective will make future supply shocks less likely and our nation's economy less vulnerable to those that occur."

—"THE FEDERAL RESERVE'S SEMIANNUAL MONETARY POLICY REPORT"; BEFORE THE SUBCOMMITTEE ON DOMESTIC AND INTERNATIONAL MONETARY POLICY OF THE COMMITTEE ON BANKING AND FINANCIAL SERVICES, U.S. HOUSE OF REPRESENTATIVES; FEBRUARY 24, 1998

"The Federal Reserve must not acquiesce in an upcreep in inflation, for acceding to higher inflation would countenance an insidious weakening of our chances for sustaining long-run economic growth. Inflation interferes with the efficient allocation of resources by confusing price signals, undercutting a focus on the longer run, and distorting incentives."

—"THE FEDERAL RESERVE'S SEMIANNUAL MONETARY POLICY REPORT"; BEFORE THE COMMITTEE ON BANKING, HOUSING, AND URBAN AFFAIRS, U.S. SENATE; FEBRUARY 26, 1997

• • •

Greenspan believes that if you see the evidence of accelerating inflation it may be too late to prevent it. He often finds himself defending the Fed's belief in preemptive actions.

"I find it ironic that our rate increases in 1994–95 were criticized by some people because inflation did not turn upward. That outcome, of course, was the intent of the tightening."

—BEFORE THE JOINT ECONOMIC COMMITTEE, U.S. CONGRESS; MARCH 20, 1997

"Those who wish for us, in the current environment, to await clearly visible signs of emerging inflation before acting are recommending we return to a failed regime of monetary policy that cost jobs and living standards.

"I wish it were otherwise, but there is no alternative to basing policy on what are, unavoidably, uncertain forecasts."
—AT THE HASKINS PARTNERS DINNER OF THE STERN SCHOOL OF BUSINESS, NEW YORK UNIVERSITY, NEW YORK CITY; MAY 8, 1997

• • •

Inflation means unsound money.

"The evidence is compelling that low inflation is necessary to the most favorable performance of the economy. Inflation, as is generally recognized throughout the world, destroys jobs and undermines productivity gains, the foundation for increases in real wages. Low inflation is being increasingly viewed as a necessary condition for sustained growth.

"It may be an old cliché, but you cannot have a vibrant growing economy without sound money. History is unequivocal on this."
—AT THE 1997 HASKINS PARTNERS DINNER OF THE STERN SCHOOL OF BUSINESS, NEW YORK UNIVERSITY, NEW YORK CITY; MAY 8, 1997

• • •

Preventing inflation is not a goal unto itself. Low inflation leads to prosperity.

"The key question is how monetary policy can best foster the highest rate of sustainable growth and avoid amplifying swings in output, employment, and prices. The historical evidence is unambiguous that excessive creation of credit and liquidity contributes nothing to the long-run growth of our productive potential and much to costly shorter-term fluctuations. Moreover, it promotes inflation, impairing the economy's longer-term potential output.

"Our objective has never been to contain inflation as an end in itself, but rather as a precondition for the highest possible long-run growth of output and income—the ultimate goal of macroeconomic policy."

—"THE FEDERAL RESERVE'S SEMIANNUAL MONETARY POLICY REPORT";
BEFORE THE COMMITTEE ON BANKING, HOUSING, AND URBAN AFFAIRS,
U.S. SENATE; JULY 22, 1997

• • •

It's difficult to know which data to study to see signs of impending inflation.

"We recognize that inflation is fundamentally a monetary phenomenon, and ultimately determined by the growth of the stock of money, not by nominal or real interest rates. In current circumstances, however, determining which financial data should be aggregated to provide an appropriate empirical proxy for the money stock that tracks income and spending represents a severe challenge for monetary analysts."

—AT THE 15TH ANNIVERSARY CONFERENCE OF THE CENTER FOR ECONOMIC
POLICY RESEARCH AT STANFORD UNIVERSITY,
STANFORD, CALIFORNIA; SEPTEMBER 5, 1997

"A re-emergence of inflation is, without question, the greatest threat to sustaining what has been a balanced economic expansion virtually without parallel in recent decades."

—BEFORE THE COMMITTEE ON THE BUDGET, U.S. HOUSE OF
REPRESENTATIVES; OCTOBER 8, 1997

• • •

Curbing inflation is the most important factor in producing a growing economy, but not the only one.

"Lower inflation and reduced budget deficits will by no means solve all of the economic problems we face. But the achievement of price stability and federal budget balance or surplus will provide the best possible macroeconomic climate in which the nation can address other economic challenges."
—BEFORE THE COMMITTEE ON BANKING, HOUSING, AND URBAN AFFAIRS, U.S. SENATE; FEBRUARY 20, 1996

• • •

Some have argued that companies grow revenues by passing along price increases to customers. Greenspan argues that during times of price stability in which companies cannot pass along increases, they must instead increase revenues through innovation—a much better situation for everyone.

"My own observation of business practices over the years suggests that the inability to pass cost increases through to higher prices provides a powerful incentive to firms to increase profit margins through innovation and greater efficiency, which boosts productivity and ultimately standards of living over time. Holding the line on inflation, thus, does not impose a speed limit on economic growth. On the contrary, it induces the private sector to focus more on efforts that yield faster long-term economic growth."
—BEFORE THE COMMITTEE ON BANKING, HOUSING, AND URBAN AFFAIRS, U.S. SENATE; JULY 18, 1996

"Markets do not always work fully to the standards of our abstract notions of perfection, that in turn rest on particular notions of the way human beings do, or should, behave in the marketplace. There appears to be general agreement among economists that the test of success of economic activity is whether, by directing an economy's scarce resources to their most productive purposes, it makes consumers as well off as is possible. Moreover, it is generally agreed that the chances of achieving these goals are greatest if prices are determined in competitive markets and reflect, to the fullest extent that is feasible, the costs in real resources of producing goods and services. While relatively straightforward to state in theory, how such a standard should be applied in practice is often subject to dispute."

—"THE EFFECTS OF MERGERS";
BEFORE THE COMMITTEE ON THE JUDICIARY,
U.S. SENATE; JUNE 16, 1998

"It is becoming increasingly evident that a key ingredient in achieving the highest possible levels of productivity, real incomes, and living standards over the long run is maintenance of price stability."

—AT THE CATHOLIC UNIVERSITY LEUVEN,
LEUVEN, BELGIUM; JANUARY 14, 1997

• • •

Monitoring inflation is a continuous activity.

"History shows clearly that given levels of resource utilization can be associated with a wide range of inflation rates. Accordingly, policymakers must monitor developments on an ongoing basis to gauge when economic potential actually is beginning to become strained—irrespective of where current unemployment rates or capacity utilization rates may lie. If we are endeavoring to fend off instability before it becomes debilitating to economic growth, direct evidence of the emerging process is essential. Consequently, one must look

beyond broad indicators to gauge the inflationary tendencies in the economy."
—BEFORE THE COMMITTEE ON FINANCE, U.S. SENATE; JANUARY 25, 1995

• • •

How do you know when you've reached the correct price for a product or service? It's becoming more difficult as we move toward a more information-based economy.

"Price stability should and will remain the central goal of our activities. But we are having increasing difficulty in pinning down the notion of what constitutes a stable price level. When industrial product was the centerpiece of the advanced economies during the first two-thirds of this century, our overall price indexes served us well. Pricing a pound of electrolytic copper presented few definitional problems. The price of a ton of cold rolled steel sheet, or a linear yard of cotton broad woven fabric, could be reasonably compared over a period of years.

"But as the century draws to a close, the simple notion of price has turned decidedly ambiguous. What is the price of a unit of software or a legal opinion? How does one evaluate the change in the price of a cataract operation over a ten-year period when the nature of the procedure and its impact on the patient has changed so radically. Indeed, how will we measure inflation, and the associated financial and real implications, in the twenty-first century when our data—using current techniques—could become increasingly less adequate to trace price trends over time?"
—AT THE CATHOLIC UNIVERSITY LEUVEN,
LEUVEN, BELGIUM; JANUARY 14, 1997

• • •

The Keynesians, who dominated economic thought for decades, believed that an economy could not have low inflation and high employment. Monetarists like Milton Friedman, Paul Volcker, and Alan Greenspan have disputed this. Greenspan has proven it.

"Over the longer run, no tradeoff is evident between inflation and unemployment. Experience both here and abroad suggests that lower levels of inflation are conducive to the achievement of greater productivity and efficiency and, therefore, higher standards of living."

—"HUMPHREY-HAWKINS, MONETARY POLICY TESTIMONY
AND REPORT TO THE CONGRESS"; FEBRUARY 22, 1994

"The strategy for monetary policy needs to be centered on making further progress toward and ultimately reaching stable prices. Price stability is a prerequisite for achieving the maximum economic expansion consistent with a sustainable external balance at high employment.

"Price stability reduces uncertainty and risk in a critical area of economic decision-making by households and businesses. In the process of fostering price stability, monetary policy also would have to bear much of the burden for countering any pronounced cyclical instability in the economy, especially if fiscal policy is following a program for multiyear reductions in the federal budget deficit."

—TESTIMONY DELIVERED BEFORE THE SENATE COMMITTEE
ON BANKING, HOUSING, AND URBAN AFFAIRS; JULY 13, 1988

"Until the late 1960s, economists often paid inadequate attention to expectations as a key determinant of inflation. Unemployment and inflation were considered simple tradeoffs. A lower rate of unemployment was thought to be associated with a higher, though constant, rate of inflation; conversely, a higher rate of unemployment was associated with a lower rate of inflation. But the experience of the past three decades has demonstrated that what appears to be a tradeoff between unemployment and inflation is quite ephemeral and misleading. Attempts to force-feed the economy beyond its potential have led in the past to rising inflation as expectations ratcheted higher and, ultimately, not to lower unemployment, but to higher unemployment, as destabilizing forces and uncertainties associated with accelerating inflation induced economic contraction.

"Lower inflation historically has been associated not just with higher levels of productivity, but with faster growth of productivity as well. Why inflation and productivity growth are linked this way empirically is not clear. To some extent higher productivity growth may help to damp inflation for a time by lessening increases in unit labor costs. But the process of cause and effect in all likelihood runs the other way as well. Lower inflation and inflation expectations reduce uncertainty in economic planning and diminish risk premiums for capital investment. They also clarify the signals from movements in relative prices, and they encourage effort and resources to be devoted to wealth creation rather than wealth preservation. Many people do not have the knowledge of, or access to, ways of preserving wealth against inflation; for them, low inflation avoids an inequitable erosion of living standards."

—"HUMPHREY-HAWKINS, MONETARY POLICY TESTIMONY
AND REPORT TO THE CONGRESS"; FEBRUARY 22, 1994

• • •

Greenspan has never promised there will never be an economic downturn or even a recession, but his goal is to limit its effects by keeping the highs lower and the lows higher.

"It is, of course, unrealistic to assume that we can eliminate the business cycle, human nature being what it is. But containing inflation and thereby damping economic fluctuations is a reasonable goal."

—"HUMPHREY-HAWKINS, MONETARY POLICY TESTIMONY
AND REPORT TO THE CONGRESS"; FEBRUARY 25, 1995

"From a longer-term perspective we have been guided by a firm commitment to contain any forces that would undermine economic expansion and efficiency by raising inflation, and we have kept our focus firmly on the ultimate goal of achieving price stability. Within that framework we have attempted not only to lean against the potential for an overheating economy, but also to cushion shortfalls in economic growth."

—AT THE 15TH ANNIVERSARY CONFERENCE OF THE CENTER
FOR ECONOMIC POLICY RESEARCH AT STANFORD UNIVERSITY,
STANFORD, CALIFORNIA; SEPTEMBER 5, 1997

• • •

Business planning will be easier if companies and consumers don't have to factor inflation into their models.

"Perhaps the most important development that has occurred in recent years has been the shift from an environment of inflationary expectations built into both business planning and financial contracts toward an environment of lower inflation. It is important that progress continue."

—STOCKHOLM, SWEDEN; APRIL 11, 1995

"The link between the control of inflation and the growth of productivity underscores the importance of providing a stable backdrop for the economy. Such an environment is especially important for an increasingly dynamic market economy, such as ours, in which technology and telecommunications are advancing rapidly. New firms, new products, new jobs, new industries, and new markets are continually being created, and they are unceremoniously displacing the old ones. The U.S. economy is a dynamic system that is always renewing itself. It is extraordinary that the system overall is as stable as it is, considering the persistent process of change in the structure of our economy."

—BEFORE THE SUBCOMMITTEE ON ECONOMIC GROWTH AND CREDIT FORMATION OF THE COMMITTEE ON BANKING, FINANCE, AND URBAN AFFAIRS, U.S. HOUSE OF REPRESENTATIVES; JULY 20, 1993

• • •

In order to stabilize the economy, President Carter believed in wage and price limits.

Q. What do you see ahead for the economy if the guidelines (wage-price guidelines proposed by Jimmy Carter) don't work?

A. My view of the outlook is actually independent of the guidelines program, since I do not believe they will be a significant factor one way or the other. I think we are moving toward a period in which the tremendous demand for credit—specifically in the mortgage market—has put inordinate pressure on the Federal Reserve to accommodate those credit demands, with the consequence that we are seeing increasing money-supply growth in the face of rapidly accelerating interest rates.

In my judgment, that is a scenario for recession. Whether it occurs in 1980 or 1979, I'm still uncertain, but I think the probability that one will occur before, say, the spring of 1980 is well in excess of 50-50.

—"PRO AND CON; WILL WAGE-PRICE GUIDELINES WORK?; NO—THERE IS A 'SCENARIO FOR RECESSION' REGARDLESS OF CARTER'S PROGRAM"; INTERVIEW WITH ALAN GREENSPAN, FORMER CHAIRMAN, COUNCIL OF ECONOMIC ADVISERS; *U.S. NEWS & WORLD REPORT*, NOVEMBER 13, 1978

Q. Can the U.S. ever get that rate down to what we used to think of as the normal rate of inflation in this country?

A. The rate has been coming down, and the reason is that the rate of increase in the money supply has been slowing. The difficulty is that if the Government attempts to curtail the rate of increase in money supply very abruptly, that will also affect employment and production.

The disinflationary policy that we are following is a gradual one, allowing the rate of increase in unit money supply to gradually ease off. The President's policies are focused on reducing inflation in a manner that does not curb the economic recovery. In fact, because inflation itself is a major cause of economic disruption, reducing inflation will help restore a full-employment economy in a balanced, non-inflationary environment.

—"WHY BUSINESS WILL CONTINUE ON THE UPSWING";
INTERVIEW WITH ALAN GREENSPAN, CHAIRMAN, COUNCIL OF
ECONOMIC ADVISERS; *U.S. NEWS & WORLD REPORT*, JUNE 28, 1976

• • •

During the late 1980s, Greenspan was credited with engineering the so-called soft landing for the economy by easing inflation down slowly. He believed that doing it quickly would lead to a recession. There was great political pressure for him to stop inflation quickly, but Greenspan held firm to his convictions that interest rates had to increase—more than 3 percentage points between March 1988 and May 1989.

At his confirmation for chairman in July 1987, Greenspan told Congress about these plans, which would follow those of his predecessor.

"I would say that the type of policies that Chairman Volcker has initiated I think are essentially on target, and I would hope, should the Senate approve me, to follow in the footsteps of those individuals who held very much that same view."

—BEFORE THE SENATE BANKING COMMITTEE;
JULY 1987

• • •

Faced with inflation, investors choose not to invest for the long term but instead hunker down in an attempt to maintain short-term gains. This is anathema to our economy because it dries up venture capital.

"The ultimate objective of economic policy is to foster the maximum sustainable rate of economic growth. This outcome depends on market mechanisms that provide incentives for economic progress by encouraging creativity, innovation, saving, and investment. Markets perform these tasks most effectively when individuals can reasonably believe that by forgoing consumption or leisure now, they can reap adequate rewards in the future. Inflation insidiously undermines such confidence. It raises doubts in people's minds about the future real value of their nominal savings and earnings, and it distorts decision-making.

"Faced with inflation, investors are more likely to divert their attention to protecting the near-term purchasing power of their wealth. Modern-day examples of economies stunted by rapid inflation are instructive. In countries with high rates of inflation, people tend to put their savings in foreign currencies and commodities rather than in the financial investments and claims on productive assets that can best foster domestic growth. By ensuring stable prices, monetary policy can play its most important role in promoting economic progress."

—BEFORE THE SENATE BANKING COMMITTEE;
FEBRUARY 1990

"If we ignore experience, we would be taking unacceptable risks of higher inflation, economic and financial instability, and, ultimately, subpar economic performance over time. We must remain alert to signs of inflationary pressures on resources. If we allow these pressures to develop, resources will begin to be used less efficiently, productivity improvements will be harder to find, and firms will be more disposed to raise prices.

"If price increases are accommodated, they can become readily embedded in higher inflation expectations. It is these expectations that make an inflationary process, once begun, difficult and expensive to reverse. As people begin to expect higher inflation, their actions to protect the purchasing power of their wages and profits add to the impetus toward accelerating prices. Experience suggests that these expectations can be turned around only slowly and with some cost to the economy's performance."

—BEFORE THE JOINT ECONOMIC COMMITTEE,
U.S. CONGRESS; DECEMBER 7, 1994

• • •

Contrary to what many may think, the goal of an inflation fighter is not zero inflation but low enough levels so companies don't have to factor it into their plans.

"Price stability does not require that measured inflation literally be zero but rather is achieved when inflation is low enough that changes in the general price level are insignificant for economic and financial planning."

—BEFORE THE COMMITTEE ON BANKING, HOUSING,
AND URBAN AFFAIRS, U.S. SENATE; FEBRUARY 19, 1993

"The goal of macroeconomic policy should be maximum sustainable growth over the long term, and evidence has continued to accumulate around the world that price stability is a necessary condition for the achievement of that goal."

—AT THE 15TH ANNIVERSARY CONFERENCE OF THE CENTER FOR ECONOMIC POLICY RESEARCH AT STANFORD UNIVERSITY, STANFORD, CALIFORNIA; SEPTEMBER 5, 1997

"Price stability is a key ingredient in maintaining the highest possible levels of productivity, real incomes, and living standards. It enables households and firms to concentrate on what they do best—produce, invest, and consume efficiently."

—BEFORE THE BOARD OF DIRECTORS, NATIONAL ASSOCIATION OF REALTORS, WASHINGTON, D.C.; MAY 16, 1995

# Greenspan on:

# The New Economy

**A**lthough credited with producing the so-called *new economy*—an economy with high employment and low inflation—Greenspan resists using that phrase. Greenspan admits, modestly perhaps, that he isn't quite sure why the economy is so good, but he is quick to add that the business cycle of boom and bust will always be present. So he prefers to use words like *virtuous cycle* to describe what he sees as the best U.S. economy ever. He offers ideas as to why he thinks the economy is doing so well, but in the end says that we won't fully understand the present economy until we look back on it in future years.

---

"It is safe to say that we are witnessing this decade, in the United States, history's most compelling demonstration of the productive capacity of free peoples operating in free markets."
—MILLENNIUM LECTURE SERIES, SPONSORED BY THE GERALD R. FORD FOUNDATION AND GRAND VALLEY STATE UNIVERSITY, GRAND RAPIDS, MICHIGAN; SEPTEMBER 8, 1999

• • •

Always the conservative thinker, Greenspan is not prone to fads.

"As a central banker, I always have great skepticism about new eras and changing structures of how the world functions."

—BEFORE THE ANNUAL CONVENTION OF THE AMERICAN SOCIETY OF
NEWSPAPER EDITORS, WASHINGTON, D.C.; APRIL 2, 1998

"One result of the more-rapid pace of innovation has been an evident acceleration of the process of 'creative destruction,' which has been reflected in the shifting of capital from failing technologies into those technologies at the cutting edge. The process of capital reallocation across the economy has been assisted by a significant unbundling of risks in capital markets made possible by the development of innovative financial products."

—"INFORMATION, PRODUCTIVITY, AND CAPITAL INVESTMENT"; BEFORE THE
BUSINESS COUNCIL, BOCA RATON, FLORIDA; OCTOBER 28, 1999

• • •

Business cycles are inevitable, but the Fed can assist in keeping them from going to the extreme.

"While bubbles that burst are scarcely benign, the consequences need not be catastrophic for the economy."

—BEFORE A JOINT ECONOMIC COMMITTEE OF CONGRESS; JUNE 17, 1999

• • •

In our new economy, measuring prices is difficult. How do you price a service or an idea? Greenspan says that our challenge is to learn how to price these intangibles because, without accurate measurements, forecasting is impossible.

"When the characteristics of products and services are changing rapidly, defining the unit of output, and thereby adjusting an item's price for improvements in quality, can be exceptionally difficult. These problems are becoming pervasive in modern economies as high tech and service prices, which are generally more difficult to measure, become ever more prominent in aggregate price measures. One does not have to look only to the most advanced technology to recognize the difficulties that are faced. To take just a few examples, automobile tires, refrigerators, winter jackets, and tennis rackets have all changed in ways that make them surprisingly hard to compare to their counterparts of twenty or thirty years ago.

". . . Although we may not be able to discern its details, the pace of change and the shift toward output that is difficult to measure are more likely to quicken than to slow down. How, then, will we measure inflation in the future if our measurement techniques become increasingly obsolete? We must keep in mind that, difficult as the problem seems, consistently measured prices do exist in principle.

". . . A Commerce Department official once compared a nation's statistical system to a tailor, measuring the economy much as a tailor measures a person for a suit of clothes—with the difference that, unlike the tailor, the person we are measuring is running while we try to measure him. The only way the system can succeed, he said, is to be just as fast and twice as agile. That is the challenge that lies ahead, and it is, indeed, a large one."

—"PRICE MEASUREMENT"; AT THE ANNUAL MEETING
OF THE AMERICAN ECONOMIC ASSOCIATION AND THE
AMERICAN FINANCE ASSOCIATION,
CHICAGO; JANUARY 3, 1998

"While there can be little doubt that major gains are being made in today's market in the quality, choice, and availability of goods and services for American consumers, it is also clear that we measure these trends rather poorly. To measure productivity and standards of living we need measures of output but, to measure output, we need to be able to define products clearly and in terms of units that do not change from one period to the next.

". . . But what is the unit of software? What is its price per unit and how does that price move from one period to the next? Also, we know that we are expending an increasing proportion of our gross domestic product denominated in current dollars on medical services. But what is the physical equivalent unit of output of medical care? What is the true price trend for the removal of cataracts, when the technology and the nature of the whole procedure is so dramatically different from what it was, say, forty or even twenty years ago? How does one price procedures when there has been a shift toward less invasive arthroscopic surgery? How does one evaluate the changed aftermath of such procedures on the day-by-day lives of patients?

"We do our best to construct overall price indexes. They may have served our purposes well in 1948, when industrial product was the centerpiece of the economy and certainly at the time of the founding of the Conference Board in 1916. But what do they tell us today? Indeed, how will we measure inflation, and the associated financial market implications, in the twenty-first century when our data—using current techniques—could become increasingly less adequate to trace price trends over time?

". . . I recognize that we are dealing with issues that have difficult metaphysical dimensions—deciding what actually constitutes the definable 'physical' or 'real' unit of a given good. Recognizing that philosophers have been addressing related questions for over two thousand years, perhaps we should not be too optimistic about reaching quick, definitive answers in all cases. But I trust that you will agree that we should encourage a good deal more research on the issue than it has received in recent years."

—AT THE 80TH ANNIVERSARY AWARDS DINNER OF THE
CONFERENCE BOARD, NEW YORK CITY; OCTOBER 16, 1996

• • •

Our economy moves so quickly that companies need sophisticated tools that rapidly determine production needs.

"A market system can approach an appropriate equilibrium only if the signals to which individual market participants respond are accurate and adequate to the needs of the adjustment process. Among the important signals are product and asset prices, interest rates, debt by maturity, detailed accounts of central banks, and private enterprises. Blinded by faulty signals, a competitive free-market system cannot reach a firm balance except by chance. In today's rapidly changing marketplace producers need sophisticated signals to hone production schedules and investment programs to respond to consumer demand."

—"RISK MANAGEMENT IN THE GLOBAL FINANCIAL SYSTEM"; BEFORE THE
ANNUAL FINANCIAL MARKETS CONFERENCE OF THE FEDERAL RESERVE
BANK OF ATLANTA, MIAMI BEACH, FLORIDA; FEBRUARY 27, 1998

• • •

The country's high-tech headquarters owe much to those who were willing to risk capital.

"Silicon Valley is a tribute both to American ingenuity and to the financial system's ever-increasing ability to supply venture capital to the entrepreneurs who are such a dynamic force in our economy."

—"THE FEDERAL RESERVE'S SEMIANNUAL MONETARY POLICY REPORT";
BEFORE THE SUBCOMMITTEE ON DOMESTIC AND INTERNATIONAL MONETARY
POLICY OF THE COMMITTEE ON BANKING AND FINANCIAL SERVICES, U.S.
HOUSE OF REPRESENTATIVES; FEBRUARY 24, 1998

• • •

Still not admitting to a new economy, Greenspan says that we have moved into uncharted territory.

"As I have indicated, this set of circumstances is not what historical relationships would have led us to expect at this point in the business expansion, and while it is possible that we have, in a sense, moved 'beyond history,' we also have to be alert to the possibility that less favorable historical relationships will eventually reassert themselves. That is why we are remaining watchful for signs of potential inflationary imbalances, even as the economy continues to perform more impressively than it has in a very long time."
—"AN UPDATE ON ECONOMIC CONDITIONS IN THE UNITED STATES";
BEFORE THE JOINT ECONOMIC COMMITTEE, U.S. CONGRESS; JUNE 10, 1998

• • •

Calling the economy "extraordinary," Greenspan notes that consumer price inflation is at an 11-year low and unemployment is at a 28-year low. He appears to be somewhat amazed by the economy's performance.

"The current economic performance, with its combination of strong growth and low inflation, is as impressive as any I have witnessed in my near half century of daily observation of the American economy."
—"AN UPDATE ON ECONOMIC CONDITIONS IN THE UNITED STATES";
BEFORE THE JOINT ECONOMIC COMMITTEE, U.S. CONGRESS, JUNE 10, 1998

• • •

No matter what kind of economic conditions we live in, human psychology remains constant. In the end, it will determine our course.

"Although there doubtless have been profound changes in the way we organize our capital facilities, engage in just-in-time inventory regimes, and intertwine our newly sophisticated risk-sensitive financial system into this process, there is one important caveat to the notion that we live in a new economy, and that is human psychology. The same enthusiasms and fears that gripped our forebears are, in every way, visible in the generations now actively participating in the American economy. Human actions are always rooted in a forecast of the consequences of those actions. When the future becomes sufficiently clouded, people eschew actions and disengage from previous commitments. To be sure, the degree of risk aversion differs from person to person, but judging the way prices behave in today's markets compared with those of a century or more ago, one is hard pressed to find significant differences. The way we evaluate assets, and the way changes in those values affect our economy, do not appear to be coming out of a set of rules that is different from the one that governed the actions of our forebears.

". . . Is there a new economy? The answer in a more profound sense is 'no.' As in the past, our advanced economy is primarily driven by how human psychology molds the value system that drives a competitive market economy. And that process is inextricably linked to human nature, which appears essentially immutable and, thus, anchors the future to the past.

". . . Whether over the past five to seven years, what has been, without question, one of the best economic performances in our history is a harbinger of a new economy or just a hyped-up version of the old, will be answered only with the inexorable passage of time. And I suspect our grandchildren, and theirs, will be periodically debating whether they are in a new economy."

—"QUESTION: IS THERE A NEW ECONOMY?"; AT THE HAAS ANNUAL BUSINESS FACULTY RESEARCH DIALOGUE, UNIVERSITY OF CALIFORNIA, BERKELEY; SEPTEMBER 4, 1998

• • •

Greenspan is a student of history and believes that we should look to the past for the future.

"Is it possible that there is something fundamentally new about this current period that would warrant such complacency? Yes, it is possible. Markets may have become more efficient, competition is more global, and information technology has doubtless enhanced the stability of business operations. But, regrettably, history is strewn with visions of such 'new eras' that, in the end, have proven to be a mirage. In short, history counsels caution."
—"THE FEDERAL RESERVE'S SEMIANNUAL MONETARY POLICY REPORT";
BEFORE THE COMMITTEE ON BANKING, HOUSING, AND URBAN AFFAIRS,
U.S. SENATE; FEBRUARY 26, 1997

"There is no evidence that the business cycle has been repealed. Another recession will doubtless occur someday, owing to circumstances that could not be, or at least were not, perceived by policymakers and financial market participants alike."
—"THE FEDERAL RESERVE'S SEMIANNUAL MONETARY POLICY REPORT";
BEFORE THE COMMITTEE ON BANKING, HOUSING, AND URBAN AFFAIRS,
U.S. SENATE; FEBRUARY 26, 1997

• • •

In 1997, Greenspan predicted that we would know in several years why the economy is doing so well. This book is being written in 2000, and he's still not sure.

"Many observers, including us, have been puzzled about how an economy, operating at high levels and drawing into employment increasingly less experienced workers, can still produce subdued and, by some measures even falling, inflation rates. It will, doubtless, be several years before we know with

any conviction the full story of the surprisingly benign combination of output and prices that has marked the business expansion of the last six years."
—"The Federal Reserve's Semiannual Monetary Policy Report";
before the Committee on Banking, Housing, and Urban Affairs,
U.S. Senate; July 22, 1997

"We do not now know, nor can anyone know, whether current developments are part of a once- or twice-in-a-century phenomenon that will carry productivity trends nationally and globally to a new, higher track, or whether we are merely observing some unusual variations within the context of an otherwise generally conventional business cycle expansion."
—"The Federal Reserve's Semiannual Monetary Policy Report";
before the Committee on Banking, Housing, and Urban Affairs,
U.S. Senate; July 22, 1997

• • •

Greenspan warns against complacency.

"The rate of growth of productivity cannot increase indefinitely. While there appears to be considerable expectation in the business community, and possibly Wall Street, that the productivity acceleration has not yet peaked, experience advises caution."
—"Growth of Economy Remarkable" by Alan Greenspan;
*National Mortgage News*, July 12, 1999

• • •

Our extraordinary economy may simply be a blip in a much larger business cycle.

"I do not say we are in a new era, because I have experienced too many alleged new eras in my lifetime that have come and gone. We are far more likely, instead, to be experiencing a structural shift similar to those that have visited our economy from time to time in the past.

"These shifts can have profound effects, often overriding conventional economic patterns for a number of years, before those patterns begin to show through again over the longer term."

—"The American Economy in a World Context"; at the 35th Annual Conference on Bank Structure and Competition of the Federal Reserve Bank of Chicago, Chicago; May 6, 1999

"I believe, at root, the remarkable generation of capital gains of recent years has resulted from the dramatic fall in inflation expectations and associated risk premiums, and broad advances in a wide variety of technologies that produced critical synergies in the 1990s."

—"State of the Economy"; before the Committee on Ways and Means, U.S. House of Representatives; January 20, 1999

• • •

Greenspan believes that we've gotten better at predicting inflation. This is one reason for the "virtuous cycle."

"Our economy has proved surprisingly robust in recent years. More rapid increases in capital spending, productivity, real wages, and asset prices have combined to boost economic growth far more and far longer than many of us would have anticipated.

"This 'virtuous cycle' has been able to persist because the behavior of inflation also has been surprisingly favorable, remaining well-contained at levels of utilization of labor that in the past would have produced accelerating prices. That it has not done so in recent years has been the result of a combination of special one-time factors holding down prices and more lasting changes in the processes determining inflation."

—before the Senate Committee on Banking, Housing, and Urban Affairs, Washington, D.C.; February 23, 1999

# Greenspan on:

# Politics

---

reenspan is a savvy political operator and understands how Washington works better than many politicians. He often finds himself in touchy political situations because the Fed, not an elected body, is subject to political oversight by Congress. The Fed board members are nominated by the president and confirmed by the Senate. Twice a year, the Fed is required by law to report to Congress on the state of the economy.

Politically, Republican Greenspan, who has served under presidents on both sides of the aisle, has battled to keep political considerations out of the Fed's decision-making process and maintain its nonpartisan, independent stance on issues. He has succeeded, winning accolades from congressional Republicans and Democrats alike.

---

Speaking with reporters after discussing the financial reform bill, Greenspan was asked if he was recommending any changes to the bill. He replied:

"My view of compromise is, if you get one, applaud and sit down."

—THE AMERICAN BANKER; MARCH 30, 1998

• • •

Many people have suggested that political considerations stand in the way of true economic reform, especially in Japan and Asia. Greenspan says that one way to counter this problem is to expose the political fallout of such actions.

"Increased transparency can counter political bias in part by exposing for all to see the risks to stability of current policies as they develop. Under such conditions, *failure* to act would also be perceived as having political costs. I suspect that recent political foot-dragging by governments in both developed and developing countries on the issue of greater transparency is credible evidence of its power and significance."
—"The Current Asia Crisis and the Dynamics of International Finance"; before the Committee on Banking and Financial Services, U.S. House of Representatives; January 30, 1998

• • •

Congress has, at times, considered a constitutional amendment requiring a balanced budget. If that happened, and Congress and the president could not agree on a budget, then the issue might be decided by the courts presided over by unelected judges. Moreover, courts don't have the proper understanding of economics to make sophisticated and complex tax and spending decisions.

"I don't like the idea of embodying concrete economic policies in the Constitution. The Constitution should be a set of principles."
—before the Senate Budget Committee; January 21, 1997

"Targeted surpluses could hopefully help to offset the in-built political bias in favor of budget deficits. I have been in too many budget meetings in the last three decades not to have learned that the ideal fiscal initiative from a political perspective is one that creates visible benefits for one group of constituents without a perceived cost to anybody else, a form of political single-entry bookkeeping."

—BEFORE THE COMMITTEE ON THE BUDGET, U.S. HOUSE OF REPRESENTATIVES; OCTOBER 8, 1997

• • •

Monetary policy succeeds only if decisions are made on the merits of economics and not politics.

"The lure of short-run gains from gunning the economy can loom large in the context of an election cycle, but the process of reaching for such gains can have costly consequences for the nation's economic performance and standards of living over the longer term. The temptation is to step on the monetary accelerator, or at least to avoid the monetary brake, until after the next election. Giving in to such temptations is likely to impart an inflationary bias to the economy and could lead to instability, recession, and economic stagnation. Interest rates would be higher, and productivity and living standards lower, than if monetary policy were freer to approach the nation's economic goals with a longer-term perspective.

"The recognition that monetary policies that are in the best long-run interest of the nation may not always be popular in the short run has led not only the United States but also most other developed nations to limit the degree of immediate control that legislatures and administrations have over their central banks. More and more countries have been taking actions to increase the amount of separation between monetary policy and the political sphere."

—BEFORE THE COMMITTEE ON BANKING, FINANCE, AND URBAN AFFAIRS, U.S. HOUSE OF REPRESENTATIVES; OCTOBER 13, 1993

• • •

Because the Fed remains independent of political whims, it can make difficult choices, such as raising interest rates, which would be unpopular in the short term and possibly political suicide for an elected official.

"There is a grudging acceptance of the degree of independence afforded our institution, and an awareness that unless we are free of the appropriations process that our independence could be compromised. It is generally recognized and appreciated that if the Federal Reserve's monetary policy decisions were subject to congressional or presidential override, short-term political forces would soon dominate. The clear political preference for lower interest rates would unleash inflationary forces, inflicting severe damage on our economy."
—AT THE ANNUAL DINNER AND FRANCIS BOYER LECTURE OF THE AMERICAN ENTERPRISE INSTITUTE FOR PUBLIC POLICY RESEARCH, WASHINGTON, D.C.; DECEMBER 5, 1996

Q: We've been through an eventful week here. We started with a Senate proposal that would have made a fairly substantial beginning on deficit reduction involving a tax increase. The president refused to accept the idea of a tax increase. Where does the week leave the budget and the budget deficit?

A: I believe it leaves it essentially where it's been for quite a significant period of time. I find last week's episode, not only with respect to questions of the deficit but with respect to the way our institutions are functioning on this issue, very frightening in a sense. We're learning that our worst fears about the inability of our institutions to function are turning out to be right. It's not that I think the president is wrong on the issue of taxes. In the longer-term sense, he is right in that the issue is really spending. Taxes are only a stopgap solution to a very much more deep-seated problem of expenditure growth.

— "An Interview with Alan Greenspan";
*The Washington Post*, Outlook, August 4, 1985

• • •

Greenspan never forgets that he serves at the pleasure of the president and Congress.

"Because the Fed is perceived as being capable of significantly affecting the lives of all Americans, that we should be subject to constant scrutiny should not come as any surprise. Indeed, speaking as a citizen, and Fed Chairman, I would be concerned were it otherwise. Our monetary policy independence is conditional on pursuing policies that are broadly acceptable to the American people and their representatives in the Congress."

—at the Annual Dinner and Francis Boyer Lecture of the
American Enterprise Institute for Public Policy Research,
Washington, D.C.; December 5, 1996

• • •

Even though Greenspan was an unofficial advisor to President Reagan at the time, he was critical of Reagan's handling of the economy.

Q. Should the President [Ronald Reagan] get more credit for reducing inflation than Chairman Paul Volcker and the Federal Reserve Board?

A. The President of the United States gets credit and blame for whatever is going on in the economy because to a very substantial extent he sets the political agenda in which other people are functioning. He will get credit for the good things and blame for the bad things, whether or not he was directly or indirectly involved.

Q. What kind of a grade would you give the President for his handling of the economy?

A. I think his philosophy is excellent. As far as implementation is concerned, I would grade him "incomplete." In other words, the course is not complete; the final exam has not been taken.

—"THE LONG-TERM BOOM NOW IN PROSPECT,"
INTERVIEW WITH ALAN GREENSPAN;
*U.S. NEWS & WORLD REPORT*, JUNE 6, 1983.
(AT THE TIME OF THIS INTERVIEW, GREENSPAN WAS HEAD OF TOWNSEND-
GREENSPAN & CO. , AN ECONOMIC CONSULTING FIRM IN NEW YORK.)

• • •

Although it has since speeded up the disclosure process, at the time of this comment, the Fed waited about six weeks before publicly disclosing monetary policy decisions. Greenspan said that without this independence from political pressure, the Fed could not do its job.

"The ability of the Federal Reserve to conduct monetary policy as it does today—with relative freedom from day-to-day pressures from the Administration as provided by Congress itself—has served the nation well over the years and should be retained."

—BEFORE THE HOUSE BANKING SUBCOMMITTEE; OCTOBER 24, 1989

• • •

Greenspan regards congressional oversight as an important part of how the Fed operates.

"The forecasting exercise can aid policymaking by helping to refine the boundaries of the likely economic consequences of our policy stance. But forecasts will often go astray to a greater or lesser degree and monetary policy has to remain flexible to respond to unexpected developments.

"A perfectly flexible monetary policy, however, without any guideposts to steer by, can risk losing sight of the ultimate goal of price stability. In this connection, the requirement under the Humphrey-Hawkins Act for the Federal Reserve to announce its objectives and plans for growth of money and credit aggregates is a very useful device for calibrating prospective monetary policy."

—TESTIMONY DELIVERED BEFORE THE SENATE COMMITTEE ON BANKING, HOUSING, AND URBAN AFFAIRS; JULY 13, 1988

• • •

In 1987, there were stories in the media and around Washington that the Department of the Treasury was running monetary policy. Greenspan, only a few months into his Fed chairmanship, had to settle the matter and establish his independence. During congressional testimony, Greenspan was asked about these rumors.

"I know of no Federal Reserve policy actions which are affected by the Treasury Department. We do not solicit their views in policy questions. We obviously try to coordinate with them in the sense that we are part of the United States government. We should not have conflicting policies with the Treasury if we can avoid it. And as best I can judge, we seem to be at the moment looking at the world at large in a similar manner, and I hope we can continue to do so.

"I mean, obviously, I can't guarantee that, but the one thing that I can assure you is that the presumption that the Treasury Department is in control of monetary policy is false."

—HOUSE BANKING SUBCOMMITTEE HEARING ON BANKING REGULATION; NOVEMBER 18, 1987

• • •

Several months later, Greenspan found himself subject to political pressure and he fought back again. In this instance, a Reagan administration official tried to persuade the Fed to reduce interest rates, a popular thing to do in an election year because it might forestall a recession that could hurt incumbent Republicans. Greenspan warned that such pressure might move the Fed to do just the opposite.

In congressional testimony, Greenspan said he had personally telephoned Treasury Secretary James A. Baker III to formally protest a letter written by Assistant Treasury Secretary Michael Darby urging the Fed to pump more money into the economy.

"I, myself, am not particularly concerned that we will be unduly influenced by the Administration . . . The only thing I hope does not happen is that the concern of our responding to political pressures gets so extraordinary that we will feel the necessity to do precisely the opposite, and we could very well be taking actions which would be counter to our best judgment."

—BEFORE THE SENATE BANKING COMMITTEE; FEBRUARY 24, 1988

# Greenspan on:

# Reputation

---

One of Greenspan's keys to success is his sound reputation. He is trusted by those in all political camps, and even though opponents may disagree with his beliefs, none has ever said he was untrustworthy or that he went back on a promise. He is an honest man.

In these excerpts, Greenspan discusses the power of a good name and its value in business.

---

Trust is the basis of all economic dealings.

"It is decidedly not true that 'nice guys finish last,' as that highly original American baseball philosopher, Leo Durocher, was once alleged to have said. I do not deny that many appear to have succeeded in a material way by cutting corners and manipulating associates, both in their professional and in their personal lives. But material success is possible in this world and far more satisfying when it comes without exploiting others. The true measure of a career is to be able to be content, even proud, that you succeeded through your own endeavors without leaving a trail of casualties in your wake.

"I cannot speak for others whose psyches I may not be able to comprehend, but, in my working life, I have found no greater satisfaction than achieving success through honest dealings and strict adherence to the view that for you to gain, those you deal with should gain as well. Human relations—be they personal or professional—should not be zero sum games. And beyond the personal sense of satisfaction, having a reputation for fair dealing is a profoundly practical virtue. We call it 'good will' in business and add it to our balance sheets.

"Trust is at the root of any economic system based on mutually beneficial exchange. In virtually all transactions, we rely on the word of those with whom we do business. Were this not the case, exchange of goods and services could not take place on any reasonable scale. Our commercial codes and contract law presume that only a tiny fraction of contracts, at most, need be adjudicated. If a significant number of businesspeople violated the trust upon which our interactions are based, our court system and our economy would be swamped into immobility."

—COMMENCEMENT ADDRESS, HARVARD UNIVERSITY,
CAMBRIDGE, MASSACHUSETTS; JUNE 10, 1999

• • •

The value of currency is really the measurement of trust in the country that issues the money.

"A nation's sovereign credit rating lies at the base of its current fiscal, monetary, and, indirectly, regulatory policy. When there is confidence in the integrity of government, monetary authorities—the central bank and the finance ministry—can issue unlimited claims denominated in their own currencies and can guarantee or stand ready to guarantee the obligations of private issuers as they see fit. This power has profound implications for both good and ill for our economies."

—AT THE CATHOLIC UNIVERSITY LEUVEN,
LEUVEN, BELGIUM; JANUARY 14, 1997

"National well-being, including material prosperity, rests to a substantial extent on the personal qualities of the people who inhabit a nation. Civilization, our civilization, rests on the presumption of a productive interaction of people engaged in the division of labor, driven by a process economists label comparative advantage. This implies mutual exchange to mutual advantage among free people."

—"Maintaining Economic Vitality"; Millennium Lecture Series, sponsored by the Gerald R. Ford Foundation and Grand Valley State University, Grand Rapids, Michigan; September 8, 1999

• • •

Trust is a vital part of free markets because consumers have choices.

"Markets enforce a degree of trust among participants that may not be so prevalent in other aspects of life. People cannot be untruthful without cost in a market context where credibility has distinct commercial value. A reputation for an inferior product might not be damaging in a centrally planned economy, but has heavy consequences in markets where choice is available."

—"The Effects of Mergers"; before the Committee on the Judiciary, U.S. Senate; June 16, 1998

# Greenspan on:
# Risk

To Greenspan, risk is a natural part of business and trade. As a regulator, he believes the Fed should not mitigate or prevent risk in the marketplace. The market and the investors themselves—not the government—should determine their own risk levels and act accordingly. However, he does believe that, in some cases, central banks should play a role in preventing large-scale economic catastrophes from spreading as well as offering a safety net for institutions that fail. How much of a safety net should be available is a subject that Greenspan ponders often because safety nets are in direct conflict with the free market concept to which he adheres.

---

Risk is an inherent aspect of creating wealth.

"Risk-taking is indeed a necessary condition for the creation of wealth. The ultimate values of all assets rest on their ability to produce goods and services in the future. And the future as we all know is uncertain and hence all investments are risky."
—BEFORE THE ANNUAL ECONOMIC SYMPOSIUM SPONSORED BY THE FEDERAL RESERVE BANK OF KANSAS CITY, JACKSON HOLE, WYOMING; AUGUST 29, 1997

"All wealth is measured by its perceived ability to produce goods and services of value in the future. Since the future is

fundamentally unknown, endeavoring to create wealth implies an uncertain expectation of how the future will unfold. That is, creating wealth is risky."
—AT THE ANNUAL MEETING AND CONFERENCE OF THE CONFERENCE OF
   STATE BANK SUPERVISORS, SAN DIEGO, CALIFORNIA; MAY 3, 1997

• • •

Safety nets should never skew free market competition.

"We must remain especially vigilant in maintaining a proper balance between a safety net that fosters economic and financial stabilization and one that benefits the competitive position of private businesses for no particular public purpose."
—BEFORE THE SUBCOMMITTEE ON FINANCIAL INSTITUTIONS AND CONSUMER
   CREDIT OF THE COMMITTEE ON BANKING AND FINANCIAL SERVICES,
   U.S. HOUSE OF REPRESENTATIVES; FEBRUARY 13, 1997

"The safety net has a tendency to benefit speculative and riskier ventures at the expense of sounder ones. Indeed, the safety net tends, other things equal, to increase the nation's overall real rate of interest by facilitating the ability of riskier borrowers to translate their potential credit demands to effective control over resources, crowding out projects that would be economic at lower real rates.

". . . The safety net, in sum, has provided measurable benefits to the U.S. economy: It has cushioned disturbances, provided flexibility, protected depositors, insulated banks from the contagion of deposit runs, and has virtually eliminated financial panics.

"But it also has had, and will continue to have, real costs. Over and above the real taxpayer costs when supervision fails to constrain the worst excesses, the safety net distorts market signals, induces managers to take on risk that does not offer the possibility of commensurate economic benefits, requires supervisors and regulators to monitor and modify behavior induced by distorted market signals, increases borrowing by riskier firms, and probably increases the real interest rate."

—AT THE FEDERAL RESERVE BANK OF CHICAGO'S ANNUAL CONFERENCE ON BANK STRUCTURE AND COMPETITION; MAY 10, 1990

• • •

Safety nets increase banks' risk tolerance, perhaps making poor judgments because they know they will be bailed out by the government. Greenspan says that if the Fed were to step in too quickly to prevent such bank failures, it runs the risk of causing large-scale economic instability.

"Banks and other private businesses recognize that to be safe against all possible risks implies a level of capital on which it would be difficult, if not impossible, to earn a competitive rate of return. On the other hand, if central banks or governments effectively insulate private institutions from the largest potential losses, however incurred, increased laxity could be costly to society as well. Leverage would escalate to the outer edge of prudence, if not beyond. Lenders to banks (as well as their owners or managers) would learn to anticipate central bank or government intervention and would become less responsible, perhaps reckless, in their practices. Such laxity would hold the potential of a major call on taxpayers. And central banks would risk inflationary instabilities from excess money creation if they acted too readily and too often to head off possible market turmoil."

—AT THE INTERNATIONAL CONFERENCE OF BANKING SUPERVISORS, STOCKHOLM, SWEDEN; JUNE 13, 1996

• • •

Theoretically, at least, the more information one has, the less risky one's activity.

"The rise in the availability of real-time information has reduced the uncertainties and thereby lowered the variances that we employ to guide portfolio decisions. At least part of the observed fall in equity premiums in our economy and others over the past five years does not appear to be the result of ephemeral changes in perceptions. It is presumably the result of a permanent technology-driven increase in infor-mation availability, which by definition reduces uncertainty and therefore risk premiums. This decline is most evident in equity risk premiums. It is less clear in the corporate bond market, where relative supplies of corporate and Treasury bonds and other factors we cannot easily identify have out-weighed the effects of more readily available information about borrowers."
—BEFORE A CONFERENCE SPONSORED BY THE OFFICE OF THE COMPTROLLER OF THE CURRENCY, WASHINGTON, D.C.; OCTOBER 14, 1999

• • •

Although speaking about banks here, Greenspan makes the point that as a general rule, risk is best if spread around.

"Recent adverse banking experiences have emphasized the problems that can arise if banks are almost the sole source of intermediation. Their breakdown induces a sharp weak-ening in economic growth. A wider range of non-bank institu-tions, including viable debt and equity markets, are important safeguards of economic activity when banking fails."
—"THE CURRENT ASIA CRISIS AND THE DYNAMICS OF INTERNATIONAL FINANCE"; BEFORE THE COMMITTEE ON BANKING AND FINANCIAL SERVICES, U.S. HOUSE OF REPRESENTATIVES; JANUARY 30, 1998

• • •

Nothing helps take the sting out of risk like having money for a rainy day.

"To the extent that policymakers are unable to anticipate or evaluate the types of complex risks that the newer financial technologies are producing, the answer, as it always has been, is less leverage, i.e. less debt, more equity, and, hence, a larger buffer against adversity and contagion."
—"The Crisis in Emerging Market Economies"; before the Committee on the Budget, U.S. Senate; September 23, 1998

"If risks associated with cross-market and cross-border securities activities are to be contained, then it is critical that large investment firms have sound internal risk monitoring and control procedures in place. Moreover, there is no substitute for strong capital positions to act as a buffer for losses."
—before the Subcommittee on Securities of the Committee on Banking, Housing, and Urban Affairs, U.S. Senate; June 14, 1989

• • •

Referring mainly to the stock market, Greenspan says that when people don't understand the risk involved, they become fearful and leave the table. It's strictly an emotional response having little to do with the true situation.

In 1998, as the dollar weathered its sharpest-ever fall against the yen, Greenspan said that in almost 50 years of monitoring the American economy, he had never witnessed investor behavior such as this.

"I've never seen anything like this. What is occurring is a broad area of uncertainty or fear. When human beings are confronted with uncertainty, meaning they do not understand the rules or the terms of particular types of engagement they're having in the real world, they disengage." (After this speech he was presented with a tape of Mahalia Jackson singing, "He's Got the Whole World in His Hands." Greenspan grimaced.)

—BEFORE THE NATIONAL ASSOCIATION OF BUSINESS ECONOMISTS;
OCTOBER 7, 1998

• • •

When assessing risk, many statisticians overlook knowledge of the markets and their customers.

"The availability of new technology and new derivative financial instruments clearly has facilitated new, more rigorous approaches to the conceptualization, measurement, and management of risk for such systems. There are limitations to the statistical models used in such systems owing to the necessity of overly simplifying assumptions. Consequently, human judgments, based on analytically less precise but far more realistic evaluations of what the future may hold, are of critical importance in risk management. Although a sophisticated understanding of statistical modeling techniques is important to risk management, an intimate knowledge of the markets in which an institution trades, and of the customers it serves, is turning out to be far more important."

—AT THE CATHOLIC UNIVERSITY LEUVEN,
LEUVEN, BELGIUM; JANUARY 14, 1997

• • •

When investors become complacent about the future, they raise their risk tolerance, a danger according to Greenspan.

"When people are exposed to long periods of relative economic tranquility, they seem inevitably prone to complacency about the future. This is understandable. We have had fifteen years of economic expansion interrupted by only one recession—and that was six years ago. As the memory of such past events fades, it naturally seems ever less sensible to keep up one's guard against an adverse event in the future."

—"THE FEDERAL RESERVE'S SEMIANNUAL MONETARY POLICY REPORT";
BEFORE THE COMMITTEE ON BANKING, HOUSING, AND URBAN AFFAIRS,
U.S. SENATE; FEBRUARY 26, 1997

• • •

When investors and companies take risks, they are moving financial progress ahead. They are more prone to take risks, and thus move toward greater prosperity, if the risk of inflation were not a factor.

"There is no way to avoid risk altogether, given the inherently uncertain outcomes of all business and household decisions. But many uncertainties and risks do not foster economic progress, and when feasible should be suppressed. A crucial risk in this category is that induced by inflation. To allow a market economy to attain its potential, the unnecessary instability engendered by inflation must be quieted."

—BEFORE THE SUBCOMMITTEE ON ECONOMIC GROWTH AND CREDIT
FORMATION OF THE COMMITTEE ON BANKING, FINANCE, AND URBAN
AFFAIRS, U.S. HOUSE OF REPRESENTATIVES; JULY 20, 1993

# Greenspan on:
# Small Business

S mall business plays a large role in the United States economy, producing newer jobs faster than its larger brethren. Small business dominates engineering, management services, and recreation industries, and in 1999 accounted for the creation of more than two and a half million new jobs.

Greenspan doesn't often have the opportunity to discuss small business concerns except in the context of credit. Borrowing money is often difficult for small businesses. The problem is especially acute for small, minority-owned businesses.

---

Greenspan joins the chorus of people who understand that small businesses often produce more innovative products than larger companies and that today's large company was yesterday's start-up.

"Nowhere in the world are the synergies of small and large businesses operating side by side in a dynamic market economy more apparent than in this country. The list of innovations by small businesses is enormous, in fields such as computer technologies, software, aerospace, pharmaceuticals, and satellite communications. And while we would be foolish to ignore the significant contributions of corporate giants, it is important to note that many of today's corporate giants were small businesses not all that long ago. America's innovative energy draws from the interaction of both large and small businesses, and will continue to do so."

—AT THE FEDERAL RESERVE SYSTEM RESEARCH CONFERENCE ON BUSINESS ACCESS TO CAPITAL AND CREDIT, ARLINGTON, VIRGINIA; MARCH 9, 1999

• • •

Many small businesses are minority-owned enterprises, which often have trouble getting financing to build and grow their businesses. Greenspan reminds us that not extending credit to these companies is discriminatory *and* bad business—not only for the prospective lender but the country as a whole.

"To the extent that market participants discriminate—consciously or, more likely, unconsciously—credit does not flow to its most profitable uses and the distribution of output is distorted. In the end, costs are higher, less real output is produced, and national wealth accumulation is slowed. By removing the non-economic distortions that arise as a result of discrimination, we can generate higher returns to human capital and other productive resources. It is important for lenders to understand that failure to recognize the profitable opportunities represented by minority enterprises not only harms these firms, it harms the lending institutions and, ultimately, robs the broader economy of growth potential. In this regard, we need to make further progress in establishing business relationships between the financial services sector and the rapidly growing number of minority- and women-owned businesses."

—AT THE FEDERAL RESERVE SYSTEM RESEARCH CONFERENCE ON BUSINESS ACCESS TO CAPITAL AND CREDIT, ARLINGTON, VIRGINIA; MARCH 9, 1999

• • •

Speaking in Los Angeles, Greenspan makes the point that start-ups often take risks that larger companies are unwilling to take. This makes the role of small companies even more important in economically depressed areas.

"Smaller banks traditionally have been an important source of credit for small businesses that do not generally have access to securities markets. In turn, small, new businesses, often employing new technology, account for much of the growth in employment in our economy. The new firms come into existence often to replace old firms that were not willing or able to take on the risks associated with high-growth strategies. This replacement of stagnating firms with dynamic new firms is at the heart of our robust, growth-oriented economy, and holds the promise of helping to revitalize areas in need such as South Central."

—"Economic Development in Low- and Moderate-income Communities"; at a Community Forum on Community Reinvestment and Access to Credit: California's Challenge, Los Angeles; January 12, 1998

# Greenspan on:

# Social Security and Medicare

The issue of social security's future is simple: Fewer young workers are paying for increasing numbers of retirees, and the gap will only increase as people live longer and continue to receive cost-of-living increases.

In the early 1980s, Alan Greenspan was chairman of the president's special commission on social security. Because the National Commission on Social Security Reform was bipartisan, many people believed that it would simply deteriorate into a political battle between Republicans and Democrats over ideology. Even Greenspan thought the effort might come to naught. Quoted in the *New York Times,* June 5, 1983, Greenspan said: "When I was asked to be the chairman, I wondered whether I had enough time to take the job on. But then I thought about it, and I thought the commission would produce a report that would sit on a shelf, and how much time could that possibly take?"

Because of his strong reputation as a fair player, and his expertise as a forecaster who always had his facts and figures checked and double-checked, the report produced by the commission in January 1983 was not relegated to a dusty shelf. Its tenets—increasing payroll taxes, postponing cost-of-living increases, and taxing some benefits—were quickly adopted by Congress.

Still, these suggestions were only a stop-gap measure. Long-term solutions have to be found and instituted.

---

The numbers of the current system simply don't add up.

"The basic premise of our current largely pay-as-you-go social security system is that future productivity growth will be sufficient to supply promised retirement benefits for current workers. However, even supposing some acceleration in long-term productivity growth from recent experience, at existing rates of domestic saving and capital investment this is becoming increasingly dubious."
—BEFORE THE COMMITTEE ON THE BUDGET, U.S. HOUSE OF
REPRESENTATIVES; OCTOBER 8, 1997

• • •

One major issue, one that will continue for many years, is whether or not to allow employees to self-direct their social security contributions, giving them a choice to place them in the stock market for example, instead of having the government invest them in Treasury bonds. Given the unpredictability of the stock market, Greenspan wonders how you forecast the rate of return with any accuracy.

"The dramatic increase in the ratio of retirees to workers that is projected, as the baby boomers move to retirement and enjoy ever greater longevity, makes our current pay-as-you-go social security system unsustainable. Furthermore, the broad support for social security appears destined to fade as the implications of its current form of financing become increasingly apparent.

"If we move now to shore up the social security program, or replace it, in part or in whole, with a private system, and

subsequently find that we had been too pessimistic in our projections, the costs to our society would be few. If we assume more optimistic scenarios and they prove wrong, the imbalances could become overwhelming, and finding a solution would be even more divisive than today's problem."
—BEFORE THE COMMITTEE ON THE BUDGET,
U.S. SENATE; JANUARY 28, 1999

• • •

Greenspan is against suggestions that the social security fund surplus, money already in the fund, be invested in stocks instead of Treasury bonds. As a dollars-and-cents issue, the numbers don't work. He argues that likely gains have been generally overstated. Shifting $600 billion of public money from bonds into equities would in itself lower the price of bonds and raise the price of equities, reducing their return.

"Investing Social Security assets in equities is largely a zero sum game. If this is indeed the case, then the net increment to the government of investing the trust fund in equities on an ongoing basis presumably would be less than the historical rates of return suggest."

His argument was not without critics. Lawrence Summers, deputy Treasury secretary, said:

"Between 1959 and 1996 the average annual rate of return earned on stocks was 3.84 percent higher than the rate earned on bonds held by the trust funds. We believe that it is important to give all Americans, even those of low and modest means, the opportunity to enjoy these potential benefits from stock market performance."
—BEFORE THE HOUSE OF REPRESENTATIVES' WAYS AND MEANS
COMMITTEE; MARCH 3, 1999

• • •

Greenspan also objected to having politicians decide where to invest social security money. He said that decisions might be motivated by politics and not sound economic reasoning.

"I do not believe that it is politically feasible to insulate such huge funds from government direction. I am fearful that we would use those assets in a way that would create a lower rate of return for social security recipients and even greater concern it would create sub-optimal use of capital and a lower standard of living."
—BEFORE THE COMMITTEE ON THE BUDGET,
U.S. SENATE; JANUARY 28, 1999

• • •

Greenspan doesn't totally close the door on partial privatization of social security, but only for new funds entering the system. He suggested a gradual approach where younger workers move to a semiprivatized plan while older workers continue in the existing one. Eventually, all workers would be covered by the new system.

"A privatized defined-contribution plan would, by definition, convert our social security system into a fully funded plan."
—BEFORE THE TASK FORCE ON SOCIAL SECURITY OF THE COMMITTEE ON
THE BUDGET, U.S. SENATE; NOVEMBER 20, 1997

• • •

One way to keep the current system viable is to make sure that cost-of-living increases are accurate. Overestimating costs will use up money more quickly than necessary. Greenspan suggested that an independent national commission be established to study the consumer price index (CPI), which Greenspan believes may be too high. Since so much government spending is based on the CPI, an accurate measure is paramount.

"This type of approach (an independent panel) would have the benefit of being objective, nonpartisan, and sufficiently flexible to take full account of the latest information . . . I think we have to separate the statistical judgments from the political judgments.

". . . There is no sharp dividing line between a pristine estimate of a price and one that is not. All of the estimates in the CPI are approximations, in some cases very rough approximations. Further, even very rough approximations can give us a far better judgment of the cost of living, than holding to a false precision of accuracy. We would be far better served following the wise admonition of John Maynard Keynes that 'it is better to be roughly right than precisely wrong.'"

—BEFORE THE COMMITTEE ON FINANCE, U.S. SENATE; JANUARY 30, 1997

• • •

Greenspan recognizes that the Medicare system has some built-in inefficiencies because it is not a truly free market enterprise. On the other hand, because of this inefficiency companies have an incentive to develop and employ new technologies to help cut costs.

"Because individuals do not pay the full incremental cost of services covered by insurance, they have less incentive to restrain the use of medical care and the adoption of technologies that divert resources from other highly valued non-medical goods and services. Indeed, there is a tendency for the insured to seek *any* medical service expected to offer at least *some* benefit, regardless of its cost in real resources. It also is

probable that this system supports the development of more new technology and greater diffusion of existing technology than would be the case were all medical care purchased directly from family resources."
—"The Allocation of the Economy's Resources Between Medicare and Competing Needs"; before the National Bipartisan Commission on the Future of Medicare; April 20, 1998

• • •

Because of Medicare's inefficient nature, does it divert the nation's resources?

"In managing Medicare, we must be particularly sensitive to the fact that, like any product, medical care is produced ultimately by the work of individuals, and the more human effort that is expended to provide medical care, the less effort that is available for making other highly valued products.

"Thus, a key question confronting this Commission is whether the current stance of public policy, lacking a market test, is altering medical demand in a way that distorts economic choices and lowers overall productivity and standards of living. If Medicare is to be sustained as a viable program, it is important that this question ultimately be answered in the negative."
—"The Allocation of the Economy's Resources Between Medicare and Competing Needs"; before the National Bipartisan Commission on the Future of Medicare; April 20, 1998

# Greenspan on:

# The Stock Market

G reenspan's words move stock markets. This has been shown several times, but most dramatically in December 1996, when he described the stock market condition as one of "irrational exuberance" and markets around the world reacted with major sell-offs. Greenspan is quite aware of the effect he has, but tries not to let it get in the way of his work toward keeping inflation in check by raising interest rates, for example. To his mind, although interest rate hikes usually make the markets drop, it's a small price to pay for a long-term, stable economy. Not all investors see it that way, however.

---

Human behavior is a main factor in how markets act. Indeed, sometimes markets act quickly, violently, with little warning.

"Ultimately, history tells us that there will be a correction of some significant dimension. I have no doubt that, human nature being what it is, that it is going to happen again and again."
—BEFORE THE COMMITTEE ON BANKING AND FINANCIAL SERVICES, U.S. HOUSE OF REPRESENTATIVES; JULY 24, 1998

"As I have indicated on previous occasions, history tells us that sharp reversals in confidence occur abruptly, most often with little advance notice. These reversals can be self-reinforcing processes that can compress sizable adjustments into a very short period. Panic reactions in the market are characterized by dramatic shifts in behavior that are intended to minimize short-term losses. Claims on far-distant future values are discounted to insignificance. What is so intriguing, as I noted earlier, is that this type of behavior has characterized human interaction with little appreciable change over the generations. Whether Dutch tulip bulbs or Russian equities, the market price patterns remain much the same.

"We can readily describe this process, but, to date, economists have been unable to *anticipate* sharp reversals in confidence. Collapsing confidence is generally described as a bursting bubble, an event incontrovertibly evident only in retrospect. To anticipate a bubble about to burst requires the forecast of a plunge in the prices of assets previously set by the judgments of millions of investors, many of whom are highly knowledgeable about the prospects for the specific investments that make up our broad price indexes of stocks and other assets."

—BEFORE A CONFERENCE SPONSORED BY THE OFFICE OF THE COMPTROLLER OF THE CURRENCY, WASHINGTON, D.C.; OCTOBER 14, 1999

• • •

Central bankers and regulators must take the value of assets in the stock market when evaluating policy.

"As the value of assets and liabilities has risen relative to income, we have been confronted with the potential for our economies to exhibit larger and perhaps more abrupt responses to changes in factors affecting the balance sheets of households and businesses. As a result, our analytic tools are going to have to increasingly focus on changes in asset values and resulting balance sheet variations if we are to understand these important economic forces. Central bankers, in particular, are going to have to be able to ascertain how changes

in the balance sheets of economic actors influence real economic activity and, hence, affect appropriate macroeconomic policies."
—"NEW CHALLENGES FOR MONETARY POLICY"; BEFORE A SYMPOSIUM
SPONSORED BY THE FEDERAL RESERVE BANK OF KANSAS CITY,
JACKSON HOLE, WYOMING; AUGUST 27, 1999

"We no longer have the luxury to look primarily to the flow of goods and services, as conventionally estimated, when evaluating the macroeconomic environment in which monetary policy must function. There are important—but extremely difficult—questions surrounding the behavior of asset prices and the implications of this behavior for the decisions of households and businesses. Accordingly, we have little choice but to confront the challenges posed by these questions if we are to understand better the effect of changes in balance sheets on the economy and, hence, indirectly, on monetary policy."
—"NEW CHALLENGES FOR MONETARY POLICY"; BEFORE A SYMPOSIUM
SPONSORED BY THE FEDERAL RESERVE BANK OF KANSAS CITY,
JACKSON HOLE, WYOMING; AUGUST 27, 1999

"In light of the importance of financial markets in the economy, and of the volatility and vulnerability in financial asset prices more generally, policymakers must continue to pay particular attention to these markets."
—BEFORE THE COMMITTEE ON WAYS AND MEANS,
U.S. HOUSE OF REPRESENTATIVES; JANUARY 20, 1999

"We do know that a significant part of the rise in [stock] prices reflects rising expected earnings and a goodly part of that is a very major change in the view of where productivity is going. What we do not know is whether it is being overdone, or to what extent it is being overdone."
—BEFORE THE HOUSE BANKING COMMITTEE; JULY 22, 1999

• • •

Although Greenspan has said he's concerned about high valuations of Internet stocks, it's not all bad.

"The size of that potential market is so huge that you have these pie-in-the-sky type of potentials for a lot of different [firms]. Undoubtedly, some of these small companies, whose stock prices are going through the roof, will succeed. And they very well may justify even higher prices. The vast majority are almost sure to fail. That's the way the markets tend to work in this regard.

"There is something else going on here though, which is a fascinating thing to watch. It is, for want of a better term, the 'lottery' principle. What lottery managers have known for centuries is that you could get somebody to pay for a one-in-a-million shot, more than the value of that chance. In other words, people pay more for a claim on a very big payoff, and that's where the profits from lotteries have always come from. But there is at root here something far more fundamental—the securities market ferreting out opportunities so capital flows to various endeavors before earnings materialize.

"That's good for our system, and that in fact—with all of its hype and craziness—is something that, at the end of the day, probably is more plus than minus."

—DURING QUESTIONS AND ANSWERS AFTER SOCIAL SECURITY HEARINGS, BEFORE THE COMMITTEE ON THE BUDGET, U.S. SENATE; JANUARY 28, 1999

• • •

Buying on the dips became a popular stock market play in the '90s, but who knows if that strategy will continue to work.

"Most of the evidence of recent years is that people who have built up 401(k)s have been the ones who have been buying on the declines and, indeed, have turned out to be prescient and wealthier. Ultimately, though, any attempt to forecast investor behavior after a correction is probably futile. Once you get a decline started, it's not clear whether people choose that as a reason to sell or to buy."

—BEFORE THE COMMITTEE ON BANKING AND FINANCIAL SERVICES, U.S. HOUSE OF REPRESENTATIVES; JULY 24, 1998

• • •

Uncertainty and complexity can breed fear.

"It has become evident time and again that when events become too complex and move too rapidly as appears to be the case today, human beings become demonstrably less able to cope. The failure of the ability to comprehend external events almost invariably induces disengagement from an activity, whether it be fear of entering a dark room, or of market volatility. And disengagement from markets that are net long, the most general case, means bids are hit and prices fall."

—BROADCAST TO THE ANNUAL MEETING OF THE SECURITIES INDUSTRY ASSOCIATION IN BOCA RATON, FLORIDA; NOVEMBER 6, 1998

• • •

This is from Greenspan's now-famous "irrational exuberance" speech, during which he hinted that he thought stock valuations were too high. Following the speech, Japan's stock market fell 3 percent, Germany's 4 percent, and America's 2 percent. Ironically, few people had even read the speech and even fewer heard anything about it.

"Clearly, sustained low inflation implies less uncertainty about the future, and lower risk premiums imply higher prices of stocks and other earning assets. We can see that in the inverse relationship exhibited by price/earnings ratios and the rate of inflation in the past. But how do we know when *irrational exuberance* has unduly escalated asset values, which then become subject to unexpected and prolonged contractions as they have in Japan over the past decade? And how do we factor that assessment into monetary policy? We as central bankers need not be concerned if a collapsing financial asset bubble does not threaten to impair the real economy, its production, jobs, and price stability. Indeed, the sharp stock market break of 1987 had few negative consequences for the economy. But we should not underestimate or become complacent about the complexity of the interactions of asset markets and the economy. Thus, evaluating shifts in balance sheets generally, and in asset prices particularly, must be an integral part of the development of monetary policy."

—AT THE ANNUAL DINNER AND FRANCIS BOYER LECTURE OF THE
AMERICAN ENTERPRISE INSTITUTE FOR PUBLIC POLICY RESEARCH,
WASHINGTON, D.C.; DECEMBER 5, 1996

• • •

The following month, Greenspan was called on the carpet by a Senate budget committee member to explain his views and also to respond to charges that he was shooting from the hip.

"It was not a shot from the hip. We thought long and in detail that any such statement could very well have immediate market effects. Our judgment, however, is that if we are endeavoring to explain, as I was in that speech, the full structure of policymaking as the Federal Open Market Committee implements it, then it would be important to make certain that everybody knows what we look at."

He added that the speech succeeded: "Everyone noticed what I was saying but people didn't read as much of the context in which that was being stated as I would have preferred."

—BEFORE THE SENATE BUDGET COMMITTEE; JANUARY 21, 1997

"History demonstrates that participants in financial markets are susceptible to waves of optimism. Excessive optimism sows the seeds of its own reversal in the form of imbalances that tend to grow over time."

—"The Federal Reserve's Semiannual Monetary Policy Report";
before the Committee on Banking, Housing, and Urban Affairs,
U.S. Senate; February 26, 1997

• • •

While the Fed's actions affect stock markets around the world, Greenspan knows that monetary policy must not focus on how the markets may react.

"While asset values are very important to the economy and so must be carefully monitored and assessed by the Federal Reserve, they are not themselves a target of monetary policy.

"We need to react to changes in financial markets, as we did this fall, but our objective is the maximum sustainable growth of the U.S. economy, not particular levels of asset prices."

—"State of the Economy";
before the Committee on Ways and Means,
U.S. House of Representatives; January 20, 1999

• • •

When it comes to investing and taking risks, human natures does not change.

"The history of large swings in investor confidence and equity premiums for rational and other reasons counsels caution in the current context. We have relearned in recent weeks that just as a bull stock market feels unending and secure as an economy and stock market move forward, so it can feel when markets contract that recovery is inconceivable.

Both, of course, are wrong. But because of the difficulty imagining a turnabout when such emotions take hold, periods of euphoria or distress tend to feed on themselves. Indeed, if this were not the case, the types of psychologically driven ebbs and flows of economic activity we have observed would be unlikely to exist. Perhaps, as some argue, history will be less of a guide than it has been in the past. Some of the future is always without historical precedent. New records are always being made. Having said all that, however, my experience of observing the American economy day by day over the past half century suggests that most, perhaps substantially most, of the future can be expected to rest on a continuum from the past. Human nature, as I indicated earlier, appears immutable over the generations and inextricably ties our future to our past."

—"QUESTION: IS THERE A NEW ECONOMY?";
AT THE HAAS ANNUAL BUSINESS FACULTY RESEARCH DIALOGUE,
UNIVERSITY OF CALIFORNIA, BERKELEY;
SEPTEMBER 4, 1998

• • •

Greenspan believes that greater market fluctuations are now a fact of life and that regulators and legislators should look to short-term fixes to prevent volatility.

"We cannot realistically hope to turn back the clock and replicate behavior of the past. Our efforts need to focus on making sure that the financial system is more resilient to shocks, rather than embarking on futile endeavors to artificially curb volatility."

—BEFORE THE HOUSE SUBCOMMITTEE ON TELECOMMUNICATIONS AND
FINANCE; MAY 19, 1988

• • •

Shortly after Greenspan took the Fed chairmanship, the stock market plunged on October 19, 1987, one of the steepest drops in history. Here, he attempts to explain the reasons, saying simply that the market was too high.

"Something had to snap. If it didn't happen in October, it would have happened soon thereafter. The immediate cause of the break was incidental. The market plunge was an accident waiting to happen."

He is unsure what the official response, if any, should have been.

"When orders exceed execution capacity, the system will break down. The only question is whether it is better for it to take the form of a controlled disruption or leave the solution to a haphazard set of forces."
—BEFORE THE SENATE BANKING COMMITTEE; FEBRUARY 2, 1988

• • •

Several years later, with hindsight, Greenspan was pleased with how the economy and the market were largely unaffected in the long term.

"The stock market crash in 1987 demonstrated quite clearly that the capacity of the financial system to absorb shocks depends critically on the robustness of payment and settlement systems."
—BEFORE THE SUBCOMMITTEE ON TELECOMMUNICATIONS AND FINANCE OF THE COMMITTEE ON ENERGY AND COMMERCE, U.S. HOUSE OF REPRESENTATIVES; MAY 25, 1994

• • •

The trend is toward international stock diversification.

"Portfolio considerations are playing an important role in the globalization of securities markets. As the welfare of people in the United States and abroad becomes increasingly dependent on the performance of foreign economies, it is natural for both individual investors and institutions to raise the share of foreign securities in investment portfolios. Such diversification provides investors a means of protecting against both the depreciation of the local currency on foreign exchange markets and the domestic economic disturbances affecting asset values on local markets. As international trade continues to expand more rapidly than global output and domestic economies become even more closely linked to those abroad, the objective of diversifying portfolios of international securities will become increasingly important. Moreover, since the U.S. dollar is still the key international currency, such diversification has been, and may continue to be, disproportionately into assets denominated in the dollar."
                              —BEFORE THE COMMITTEE ON WAYS AND MEANS,
                    U.S. HOUSE OF REPRESENTATIVES; JANUARY 25, 1990

• • •

One suggestion for keeping market valuations from getting out of hand is to raise margin requirements. Here, Greenspan discusses the pros and cons.

SEN. CHARLES SCHUMER (D—New York): Why not raise margin requirements as a way of making sure that stock market increases do not get so far ahead that a bubble might burst? Why haven't you done it? What is your objection to it, and what would be an alternative strategy?

GREENSPAN: The reason over the years that we have been reluctant to use the margin authorities which we currently have, is that all studies have suggested that the level of stock prices has nothing to do with margin requirements. There is no evidence to suggest that changes in margin requirements . . . have any effect on prices.

Secondly, we have been reluctant to move margin requirements, which clearly would have no effect on large investors whose means of financing go far beyond the usual means in which brokers extend credit. And we have been quite reluctant to see restraints on specific individuals and not on others. It is certainly the case that the numbers that you cite, especially for November and December, have caught our attention, and moved up to a pace which has created a good deal of evaluation on our part and obviously of the supervisory regulators. There has been considerable conversation going on with respect to addressing this issue because it goes beyond the mere issue of stocks. It goes into initial margins and maintenance margins relevant to futures markets, options and other instruments that are related to this particular area. I can't say where this particular endeavor on our part is going to come out, but it's fairly evident that we have observed the same phenomenon and we have been speaking to the same people you have been speaking to.

SEN. SCHUMER: You're worried?

GREENSPAN: Obviously. If we were not worried we would not be engaged in trying to understand the process.

SEN. SCHUMER: Is there an alternative to raising the margin requirements?

GREENSPAN: We have also been discussing what alternatives there are, and it's very easy to invent all sorts of new schemes that are allegedly going to do something, and when put into place turn out to be less than perfect. I don't want to suggest we're about to do anything at this stage, but I would confirm we are obviously going to do a great deal of thinking about the whole process.

—BEFORE THE SENATE BANKING COMMITTEE;
JANUARY 26, 2000

# Greenspan on:
# Technology

---

Greenspan is a believer in technology and its power to shape economic prosperity. He notes how technology has shrunk the size of manufactured products, making them easier to transport. Indeed, technology has shifted the focus of our economy from hard goods to ideas. Another facet of technology that he highlights in many of his presentations is how technology allows companies to substitute capital for labor. This, according to Greenspan, opens up new possibilities but also, unfortunately, puts unskilled people out of work.

---

"The newer technologies have made capital investment distinctly more profitable, enabling firms to substitute capital for labor far more productively than they would have a decade or two ago."
—"The Federal Reserve's Semiannual Report On Monetary Policy": before the Committee on Banking, Housing, and Urban Affairs, U.S. Senate; February 23, 1999

• • •

Much of our prosperity stems from using technology to better manage manufacturing and shipping of processes.

"Over the last century, for example, the rate of increase of the gross domestic product in the United States, adjusted for price change—our measure of gains in the real value of output—has averaged around three percent per year. Only a small fraction of that represents growth in the tonnage of physical materials—oil, coal, ores, wood, raw chemicals, for example. The remainder represents new insights into how to rearrange those physical materials to better serve human needs. This process has enabled valued goods to be transported more easily and to be produced with ever fewer workers, allowing the more efficient division of labor to propel overall output and standards of living progressively higher."

—AT THE 81ST ANNUAL MEETING
OF THE AMERICAN COUNCIL ON EDUCATION,
WASHINGTON, D.C.; FEBRUARY 16, 1999

"Although many forces have been at play, this surge in competitive trade has clearly owed, in large part, to significant advances in technological innovation."

—BEFORE THE DALLAS AMBASSADORS FORUM,
DALLAS, TEXAS;
APRIL 16, 1999

• • •

Information technology has radically changed the way we do business, but it has not made forecasting future events any more certain.

"I have hypothesized on a number of occasions that the synergies that have developed, especially among the microprocessor, the laser, fiber optics, and satellite technologies, have dramatically raised the potential rates of return on all types of equipment that embody or utilize these newer technologies. But beyond that, innovations in information technology—so-called IT—have begun to alter the manner in which we do business and create value, often in ways that were not readily foreseeable even five years ago.

"As this century comes to an end, the defining characteristic of the current wave of technology is the role of information. Prior to this IT revolution most of twentieth century business decisionmaking had been hampered by limited information. Owing to the paucity of timely knowledge of customers' needs and of the location of inventories and materials flows throughout complex production systems, businesses required substantial programmed redundancies to function effectively. Doubling up on materials and people was essential as backup to the inevitable misjudgments of the real-time state of play in a company. Decisions were made from information that was hours, days, or even weeks old. Accordingly, production planning required costly inventory safety stocks and backup teams of people to maintain quality control and to respond to the unanticipated and the misjudged.

"Large remnants of information void, of course, still persist, and forecasts of future events on which all business decisions ultimately depend are still unavoidably uncertain. But the recent years' remarkable surge in the availability of real-time information has enabled business management to remove large swaths of inventory safety stocks and worker redundancies, and has armed firms with detailed data to fine-tune product specifications to most individual customer needs."

—"High-tech Industry in the U.S. Economy"; before the Joint Economic Committee, U.S. Congress; June 14, 1999

"The use of information in business decision-making can be best described as an effort to reduce the fog surrounding the future outcomes of current decisions. Because the future is never entirely predictable, risk in any business action committed to the future—that is, virtually all business actions—can be reduced but never eliminated. Information technologies have improved our real-time understanding of production processes, reducing the degree of uncertainty and, hence, risk. This, in turn, has lessened the need for a whole series of programmed redundancies from which, in the end, little to no productive capability is achieved. In short, information technology raises output per hour in the total economy by reducing hours worked on activities needed to guard productive processes against the unknown and the unanticipated. Narrowing the uncertainties reduces the number of hours required to maintain any given level of readiness."

—"INFORMATION, PRODUCTIVITY, AND CAPITAL INVESTMENT";
BEFORE THE BUSINESS COUNCIL, BOCA RATON, FLORIDA;
OCTOBER 28, 1999

"History is strewn with projections of technology that have fallen wide of the mark. There is little reason to believe that we are going to be any better at this in the future than in the past."

—BEFORE A JOINT ECONOMIC COMMITTEE OF CONGRESS; JUNE 14, 1999

• • •

We can't predict which technologies will pay off and which will not, so we must become even more flexible in our thinking.

"Our future entrepreneurs must be prepared to compete in an environment in which the largest part of the growth in output is the result of new insights. Breakthroughs in technology are continually adding to the ever-longer list of wholly conceptual elements in our economic output. The success of our future business leaders will depend greatly on their capacity to develop and apply new technology and to rearrange physical reality to achieve products and services more highly valued by consumers. To do this will demand

not only greater specialized knowledge, but also an ability to deal with risk and uncertainty. Unfortunately, we have found that we never can predict with any precision which particular technology or synergies of technologies will add significantly to our knowledge and our ability to gain from that knowledge."
—"The Underemployment of Minorities"; at the Wall Street Project Anniversary Conference of the Rainbow/PUSH Coalition, New York; January 16, 1998

• • •

The shifting of movements and demand are now following the flows of information.

"New technology has radically reduced the costs of borrowing and lending across traditional national borders, facilitating the development of new instruments and drawing in new players. One result has been a massive increase in capital flows. Information is transmitted instantaneously around the world, and huge shifts in the supply and demand for funds naturally follow."
—before the Annual Financial Markets Conference of the Federal Reserve Bank of Atlanta, Miami Beach, Florida; February 27, 1998

• • •

A downside of technology is that it gives single individuals power to engage in massive transactions.

"The collapse of Barings Brothers in 1995 showed how much more rapidly losses can be generated in the current environment relative to a century earlier when Barings Brothers confronted a similar episode. Current technology enables single individuals to initiate massive transactions with very rapid execution. Clearly, not only has the productivity of

global finance increased markedly, but so, obviously, has the ability to generate losses at a previously inconceivable rate."
—AT THE CATHOLIC UNIVERSITY LEUVEN,
LEUVEN, BELGIUM; JANUARY 14, 1997

"One lesson we have clearly learned is that we never can predict with any precision which particular technology or synergies of technologies will add significantly to our knowledge and ability to gain from that knowledge."
—AT THE BUILDING DEDICATION CEREMONIES AT THE KENAN-FLAGLER
BUSINESS SCHOOL, UNIVERSITY OF NORTH CAROLINA, CHAPEL HILL;
SEPTEMBER 12, 1997

"Over the past century, by far the smallest part of the growth in America's real gross domestic product reflects increased physical product measured in bulk or weight. Most of our gains have been the result of new insights into how to rearrange physical reality to achieve ever-higher standards of living."
—AT THE BUILDING DEDICATION CEREMONIES AT THE KENAN-FLAGLER
BUSINESS SCHOOL, UNIVERSITY OF NORTH CAROLINA, CHAPEL HILL;
SEPTEMBER 12, 1997

"The most important single characteristic of the changes in U.S. technology in recent years is the ever expanding conceptualization of our Gross Domestic Product. We are witnessing the substitution of ideas for physical matter in the creation of economic value—a shift from hardware to software, as it were."
—AT THE ANNUAL CONVENTION OF THE AMERICAN BANKERS ASSOCIATION,
BOSTON; OCTOBER 5, 1997

• • •

Distance is becoming less of a factor in the cost of transporting knowledge and information.

"Increasingly, the physical distance between communications endpoints is becoming less relevant in determining the difficulty and cost of transporting information. Once fiber-optic and satellite technologies are in place, the added resource cost of another 200 or 2,000 miles is often quite trivial. As a consequence, the movement of inputs and outputs across geographic distance is progressively becoming a smaller component of overall business expenses, particularly as intellectual—and therefore immaterial—products become proportionately more important in the economy. This enables an average business firm to broaden markets and sales far beyond its original domicile. Accordingly, fixed costs are spread more widely. For the world market as a whole, the specialization of labor is enhanced to the benefit of standards of living of all market participants."

—BEFORE THE COMMITTEE ON BANKING, HOUSING, AND URBAN AFFAIRS, U.S. SENATE; FEBRUARY 20, 1996

"Most people only have rudimentary skills when it comes to making computers do what they want."

—BEFORE THE INDEPENDENT BANKERS ASSOCIATION OF AMERICA ANNUAL CONVENTION, NEW ORLEANS; MARCH 18, 1996

# Greenspan on:

# Trade

T o Alan Greenspan, free trade is paramount if national and world economies are to function efficiently. His ideal situation is for barriers to be lowered, allowing free markets to take over.

Global trade is a growing trend.

"One of the most impressive and persistent trends of the last half century is the expansion of international trade. Adjusted for price change, trade across national borders has increased fourteenfold—far faster than the fivefold increase in world GDP."

—BEFORE THE DALLAS AMBASSADORS FORUM, DALLAS, TEXAS; APRIL 16, 1999

• • •

Interestingly, even if one nation lowers its trade barriers, it benefits no matter what other countries do.

"If trade barriers are lowered by both parties, each clearly benefits. But if one lowers barriers and the other does not, the country that lowered barriers unilaterally would still be better off having done so. Raising barriers to achieve protectionist equality with reluctant trading partners would be neither to our benefit, nor to theirs. The best of all possible worlds for competition is for both parties to lower trade barriers. The worst is for both to keep them up."

—BEFORE THE DALLAS AMBASSADORS FORUM,
DALLAS, TEXAS; APRIL 16, 1999

• • •

Free trade goes beyond job creation.

"We try to promote free trade on the mistaken ground that it will create jobs. The reason should be that it enhances standards of living through the effects of competition on productivity."

—AT THE COMMONWEALTH CONFERENCE ON INTERNATIONAL BUSINESS,
BOSTON; JUNE 2, 1999

• • •

Protectionist polices can only hurt us.

"By joining with our major trading partners and international financial institutions in helping to stabilize the economies of Asia and promoting needed structural changes, we are also encouraging the continued expansion of world trade and global economic and financial stability on which the ongoing increase of our own standards of living depends. If we were to cede our role as a world leader, or backslide into protectionist policies, we would threaten the source of much of our own sustained economic growth."

—"THE FEDERAL RESERVE'S SEMIANNUAL MONETARY POLICY REPORT";
BEFORE THE SUBCOMMITTEE ON DOMESTIC AND
INTERNATIONAL MONETARY POLICY OF THE
COMMITTEE ON BANKING AND FINANCIAL SERVICES,
U.S. HOUSE OF REPRESENTATIVES; FEBRUARY 24, 1998

• • •

Antidumping campaigns are often a ruse to prevent competition.

"The campaign to expand free trade is never won. It is a continuing battle. While tariffs in industrial countries have come down sharply over the past half century, other barriers have become more prevalent. Administrative protection in the form of antidumping suits and countervailing duties is a case in point. While these forms of protection have often been imposed under the label of promoting 'fair trade,' oftentimes they are just simple guises for inhibiting competition. Typically, antidumping duties are levied when foreign average prices are below average cost of production. But that also describes a practice that often emerges as a wholly appropriate response to a softening in demand. It is the rare case that prices fall below marginal cost, which would be a more relevant standard. Antidumping initiatives should be reserved, in the view of many economists, for those cases where anti-competitive behavior is involved. Contrary to popular notions about antidumping suits, under U.S. and WTO law, it is not required to show evidence of predatory behavior, or intention to monopolize, or of any other intentional efforts to drive competitors out of business."

—BEFORE THE DALLAS AMBASSADORS FORUM,
DALLAS, TEXAS; APRIL 16, 1999

• • •

As we move toward an information or knowledge-based economy, world trade will become dominated by intangible items crossing borders. These intangibles move faster and with greater ease than manufactured goods.

"This surge in cross-border financial transactions has paralleled a large advance in the magnitude of cross-border trade of goods and services. A key factor behind these trends in international trade and securities transactions is a process that I have described elsewhere as the 'downsizing of economic output.' The creation of economic value has shifted increasingly toward conceptual values with decidedly less reliance on physical volumes. Today, for example, major new insights have led to thin fiber optics, replacing vast tonnage of copper in communications. Financial transactions historically buttressed with reams of paper are being progressively reduced to electronic charges. Such advances not only reduce the amount of human physical effort required in making and completing financial transactions across national borders but facilitate more accuracy, speed, and ease in execution.

"Underlying this process have been quantum advances in technology, spurred by economic forces. In recent years, the explosive growth in information-gathering and processing techniques has greatly extended our analytic capabilities of substituting ideas for physical volume. The purpose of production of economic value will not change. It will continue to serve human needs and values. But the form of output increasingly will be less tangible and hence more easily traded across international borders. It should not come as a surprise therefore that in recent decades the growth in world trade has far outstripped the growth in domestic demand. As a necessary consequence, imports as a share of output, on average, have risen significantly. Since irreversible conceptual gains are propelling the downsizing process, these trends almost surely will continue into the twenty-first century and beyond."

—BEFORE THE COMMITTEE ON WAYS AND MEANS,
U.S. HOUSE OF REPRESENTATIVES; JANUARY 25, 1990

"As technology continues to downsize the products we produce, thereby lowering transportation costs, growth in the cross-border volume of trade in goods will surely continue to outstrip growth in real world GDP. Trade in services will doubtless increase even more. The financing of expanding cross-border merchandise trade and the rapid development of accompanying arbitrage and risk dispersion suggest a far larger world financial system than currently exists. If we can resist protectionist pressures in our societies, we can look forward to the benefits of the international division of labor on a much larger scale in the twenty-first century."

—"INTERNATIONAL FINANCIAL INTEGRATION"; DELIVERED BEFORE THE
FEDERATION OF BANKERS ASSOCIATIONS OF JAPAN, TOKYO;
OCTOBER 14, 1992

• • •

Greenspan expresses concern about the growing trade imbalance, in which more goods and services are being bought from outside the U.S. compared to U.S. exports. For our economy to remain healthy, this situation must change. Increased agricultural exports could help.

SEN. WAYNE ALLARD (R–Colorado): Do you have any concerns about the current trade balance?

GREENSPAN: The current trade balance is being engendered at this point by, one, the incredible rise in demand domestically in the United States and, indirectly and in a related sense, by the very high rates of return available on new technologies that are emerging in this country, which has attracted a very substantial amount of investment in the United States. Since the current account deficit is a broader concept of the trade deficit, the current account deficit must also be equal to the amount of capital flows into the United States.

Indeed, if there is an imbalance between the demand for capital and the supply of capital, it's that which causes the dollar's foreign exchange value to change. In view of the fact that the exchange value of the dollar has been relatively flat for quite a while, it is suggestive that both forces are at play here. That is, the significant increase in imports is being driven by the demand that has been in part created by the so-called wealth effect. But the capital inflow is also indirectly created by the same forces that create the wealth effect, namely the very high rates of return on new capital. Over the very long run, it is probably not credible to presume that we can continue a current account deficit or trade imbalance at the levels we currently have because it obviously means that our net debt or the net claims on the United States by foreigners is accumulating, because indeed the current account deficit is basically the net change in the debt. And ultimately, the interest service on that very large external debt will create serious problems. So that everyone who looks at this process knows that somewhere—it could be an extraordinary number of years, possibly, I don't really know, and I don't think anyone else knows—but it is true that it cannot persist indefinitely. The question is, what are the forces which will eventually bring it down? One of the things that in the short run would clearly be very effective is an acceleration of growth abroad and an increase in our export markets. This gets to the issue that the chairman raised with agriculture earlier, because should that occur, our exports would increase and our trade imbalance would narrow as a consequence."

—BEFORE THE SENATE BANKING COMMITTEE; JANUARY 26, 2000

# Some of Greenspan's Nonrandom Thoughts

For a different person, this section might be called "random thoughts," but Alan Greenspan's public comments are never random. They are always calculated, precise, and thoughtful. Following are topics that are not included in other sections.

## On Taxation

A reduction in capital gains taxes has been a hot issue in Congress for a long time. Greenspan believes that such reduction would not affect tax revenues but might adversely affect the budget deficit in the short term.

"Although the empirical evidence is admittedly mixed, I strongly suspect that the elimination of, or a major reduction in, the rate of taxation on capital gains would entail little, if any, loss of total tax revenue over the long run. However, it is currently not possible to estimate with any degree of precision the impact of such a proposal on the deficit within the horizon of the current budget process."

—BEFORE A JOINT HEARING OF THE SENATE AND HOUSE
COMMITTEES ON THE BUDGET; JANUARY 10, 1995

"The capital gains tax is more an issue of the incentive to invest than a creation of savings. I've always argued that taxation of capital is the poorest means of creating revenue, if the long-term growth and stability of the economy is the criterion we employ to make the judgment. I would not argue that the capital gains tax has a material effect on the savings rate. It may, but I've seen no strong evidence to suggest it does. I surely would not use that as the reason for trying to reduce it."

—BEFORE THE SENATE BANKING COMMITTEE; JANUARY 26, 2000

# On Consumer Issues

It's impossible to make forecasts without the proper data. One such piece of missing information is the value that consumers place on their time.

"We should move to improve our understanding of the value that consumers place on their own time. Absent such knowledge, it will be impossible for the BLS [Bureau of Labor Statistics] to estimate the value of many goods and services that mainly serve to enhance convenience and save time. We will have to attempt to build an understanding of why consumers shop at the places they do: What characteristics of an outlet are important, and how much so? Location, hours of operation, inventory, and quality of service all are likely influences on the value that consumers place on their shopping experience, and all will be important in helping the BLS to develop a more sophisticated statistical method for dealing with the appearance of new consumer outlets, including those that operate over the Internet."

—BEFORE THE COMMITTEE ON FINANCE, U.S. SENATE; JANUARY 30, 1997

# On Consumer Debt

The total amount of consumer debt is not as important as the ability to service such debt.

"The concerns that you [Sen. Christopher Dodd, (D–Connecticut] have with respect to the level of consumer debt are valid, although it must be viewed in the context of changing the structure of the debt. Debt service burdens however—meaning the percentage of cash that people pay out as a percentage of income—has really not gone up all that much, in part it's because of the lower interest rates that have occurred, and in many instances the extended maturities of various different types of instruments, which has kept the level of payments down. Obviously home equity loans displacing credit card debt has had the effect of lowering the annual debt service charge, so that we have very high debt. But it is not yet something which creates concerns as far as the economy overall is concerned."

—BEFORE THE SENATE BANKING COMMITTEE; JANUARY 26, 2000

# On Money in General

"For, at root, money—serving as a store of value and medium of exchange—is the lubricant that enables a society to organize itself to achieve economic progress. The ability to store the fruits of one's labor for future consumption is necessary for the accumulation of capital, the spread of technological advances and, as a consequence, rising standards of living."

—AT THE ANNUAL DINNER AND FRANCIS BOYER LECTURE
OF THE AMERICAN ENTERPRISE INSTITUTE FOR
PUBLIC POLICY RESEARCH, WASHINGTON, D.C.;
DECEMBER 5, 1996

# On Privacy

Greenspan makes the point that concern over privacy may be one reason why more consumers don't use electronic transactions, especially credit cards and ATM transfer. Overwhelmingly, cash is still the most-used means of payment.

"Given choices in the marketplace that include price, quality and differing degrees of privacy, I have little doubt that privacy would be valued and sought after. In the financial sphere, the payment systems of the United States present a paradox. Our systems, and banking arrangements, for handling high-value dollar payments are all electronic and have been for many years. Banking records, including those for loans and deposits, have been computerized since the 1960s. Securities markets also now rely on highly automated records and systems, born out of necessity following the paperwork crisis of the 1970s.

"Thus, it might seem strange that in transactions initiated by consumers, paper—currency and checks—remains the payment system of choice. Debit and ATM cards, along with automated clearing house payments, account for a very small percentage of transactions. Even the use of popular credit cards has only recently begun to challenge paper's dominance. While there are many other factors involved in this anomaly, the value of privacy of transaction has clearly been a significant determinant."

—AT THE CONFERENCE ON PRIVACY IN THE INFORMATION AGE, SALT LAKE CITY, UTAH; MARCH 7, 1997

# On Productivity

A better way to measure productivity:

"I've always been of the opinion that if you really want to know what's happening with productivity, you have to do it from the income side because the data on profits are good, the data on prices are reasonably good, and all the unit costs are a better measure to get the fallout. If you have unit labor costs and some varying judgments of what's going on in compensation per hour, obviously productivity comes out as a residual. And it is a far more consistent story about what's going on in the world to reconcile the fact that, despite increasing compensation per hour, prices have done nothing. The only way in the full accounting system that that can happen is to say that productivity growth has accelerated in recent years, and indeed, all the collateral evidence does suggest that that is indeed the case."

—BEFORE THE 40TH ANNUAL MEETING OF THE NATIONAL ASSOCIATION OF BUSINESS ECONOMISTS, WASHINGTON, D.C.; OCTOBER 3–7, 1998

# On Mergers

Although referring to banks mainly, Greenspan says that companies often spurn merger offers out of management ego with lack of regard for shareholders' interests.

"Let's remember when we talk about hostile takeovers that the hostility is between the managements of these two organizations, not between the shareholders of either. In fact, the problem that exists is that, too often in my judgment, the managements try to protect themselves from, in effect, their own shareholders."

—BEFORE THE SENATE BANKING COMMITTEE; FEBRUARY 24, 1988

# On Management

"It is difficult to prove, but 'luck,' the great random leveler in the marketplace, appears to play an ever smaller role in determining success and failure in today's just-in-time, high-quality, productive systems. Those systems appear to be especially rewarding to financial skills."

—BEFORE THE ANNUAL CONVENTION OF THE AMERICAN SOCIETY OF NEWSPAPER EDITORS, WASHINGTON, D.C.; APRIL 2, 1998

# On Regulation

Markets are better off regulating themselves without intrusion from government.

"It is critically important to recognize that no market is ever truly unregulated. The self-interest of market participants generates private market regulation. Thus, the real question is not whether a market should be regulated. Rather, the real question is whether government intervention strengthens or weakens private regulation. If incentives for private market regulation are weak or if market participants lack the capabilities to pursue their interests effectively, then the introduction of government regulation may improve regulation. But if private market regulation is effective, then government regulation is at best unnecessary. At worst, the introduction of government regulation may actually weaken the effectiveness of regulation if government regulation is itself ineffective or undermines incentives for private market regulation."

—AT THE FINANCIAL MARKETS CONFERENCE OF THE FEDERAL RESERVE BANK OF ATLANTA, CORAL GABLES, FLORIDA; FEBRUARY 21, 1997

"We should not lose sight of the fact that government regulation, if not carefully designed, can undermine the effectiveness of private market regulation and can itself be ineffective in protecting the public interest. No market is ever truly unregulated in that the self-interest of participants generates private market regulation. Counterparties thoroughly scrutinize each other, often requiring collateral and special legal protections; self-regulated clearing houses and exchanges set margins and capital requirements to protect the interests of the members. Thus, the real question is not whether a market should be regulated. Rather, it is whether government intervention strengthens or weakens private regulation, and at what cost. At worst, the introduction of government rules may actually weaken the effectiveness of regulation if government regulation is itself ineffective or, more importantly, undermines incentives for private market regulation. Regulation by government unavoidably involves some element of perverse incentives, that is, moral hazard. If private market participants believe that government is protecting their interests, their own efforts to do so will diminish."

—AT THE SPRING MEETING OF THE INSTITUTE OF INTERNATIONAL FINANCE, WASHINGTON, D.C.; APRIL 29, 1997

"As we move into a new century, the market-stabilizing private regulatory forces should gradually displace many cumbersome, increasingly ineffective government structures. This is a likely outcome since governments, by their nature, cannot adjust sufficiently quickly to a changing environment, which too often veers in unforeseen directions.

"The current adult generations are having difficulty adjusting to the acceleration of the uncertainties of today's silicon driven environment. Fortunately, our children appear to thrive on it. The future accordingly looks bright."

—AT THE ANNUAL CONFERENCE OF THE ASSOCIATION OF PRIVATE
ENTERPRISE EDUCATION, ARLINGTON, VIRGINIA; APRIL 12, 1997

# On the Euro's Success

"The introduction of the euro is clearly going to significantly alter reserve holdings. As markets for euro-denominated assets develop, the euro should become increasingly attractive as a world reserve currency. The bid-ask spreads on average of, say, the separate currency government bonds of the Euro-II countries before January 1, were wider than the spreads on average that should eventually emerge for new euro-denominated issues. Such increased liquidity should reduce the cost of holding reserves, though conceivably the credit risk of bonds, not denominated in a currency fully controlled by a domestic central bank, would rise. To some extent the increased attractiveness of the euro should reduce the demand for dollars. But history suggests that this effect is likely to be limited and evolutionary."

—BEFORE THE WORLD BANK CONFERENCE ON RECENT TRENDS IN RESERVE
MANAGEMENT, WASHINGTON, D.C.; APRIL 29, 1999

# On the Ever-Changing Value of the Dollar

"It is important to remember that it is the rate of change of the dollar's exchange rate, not its levels, that affects the rate of price inflation and interest rates [in the United States]. If the adjustment to a lower exchange value of the dollar is dragged out, it is possible to reach a new balance without setting off a further destabilizing run-up in either interest rates or consumer prices. A sharply falling dollar, however, would, by pushing interest rates markedly higher, tilt the economy downward, accelerating inflation and perhaps even altering the ultimate equilibrium value of the dollar. Economic policymakers both in the United States and elsewhere are, accordingly, in a very difficult position. If they announce a goal of gradual dollar devaluation, the market will produce that level immediately, with all its adverse consequences. If they announce that the current level is the right one, they are going to have a tough time enforcing it."

—DURING A PUBLIC BROADCASTING SYSTEM TELEVISION NEWS PROGRAM;
APRIL 20, 1987

# What Others Say about Alan Greenspan

D espite Greenspan's modest demeanor in public, friends and acquaintances paint him as a kind, funny, utterly charming person in private. He is a sought-after party guest and often makes the rounds at Washington galas.

Although he doesn't give interviews, those who know him are less constrained about his finer points.

---

In July 1999, Senate Republicans pushed for the biggest tax cuts in 20 years despite strong public opposition from Greenspan, who repeated his call to pay off the national debt with any budget surpluses. Republican senators ignored his strongly worded recommendations, prompting Sen. Daniel Patrick Moynihan (D–New York) to say:

"Mr. Greenspan is treated well on Capitol Hill, but it appears Republicans do not want to heed his advice."

• • •

Some say that those in Washington are getting used to interpreting Greenspan's sometimes deliberately ambiguous remarks to their advantage.

"Alan Greenspan's statements have become like the Bible. Nobody reads them very closely and everybody quotes them.

And they quote him on both sides of the argument," joked Sen. Phil Gramm (R–Texas).

—AT A SENATE BUDGET COMMITTEE HEARING; JULY 28, 1999

• • •

In June 1999, it was reported in *Newsweek* that the Secret Service was asked to protect Alan Greenspan in response to threats.

"Investors would be very upset if suddenly Alan Greenspan didn't come to work for some reason."

—DAN LAUFENBERG, ECONOMIST AT AMERICAN EXPRESS FINANCIAL ADVISORS

"There used to be a slogan that said, 'When E. F. Hutton talks, people listen.' "Well, these days it's 'When Alan Greenspan talks, people listen.'"

—ROBERT M. RUBIN,
SENIOR VICE PRESIDENT AND CIO AT
ELF ATOCHEM NORTH AMERICA, IN PHILADELPHIA;
*INFOWORLD*, MAY 24, 1999

• • •

One of the funniest comments came from presidential candidate Sen. John McCain during a debate in New Hampshire. The Republican candidates were asked if they would reappoint Greenspan to another term as Fed Chairman.

MR. HUME (Britt Hume, Correspondent, Fox TV News): Senator McCain, where do you come out on this question of this stock market, as high as it is, and on the issues that have just been asked of Mr. Forbes relating to Mr. Greenspan, who seems, at times, alarmed by the level of the stock market? Do you think it's a bubble? Do you think we should be afraid of this?

SEN. McCAIN: I share Mr. Greenspan's concern. And, by the way, I would not only reappoint Mr. Greenspan; if Mr. Greenspan should happen to die, God forbid, I would do like they did in the movie *Weekend at Bernie's*. I'd prop him up and put a pair of dark glasses on him and keep him as long as we could. (Laughter.)

The fact is that Mr. Greenspan deserves great credit—great credit—for this economic recovery. He's been a steady hand. He's unintelligible, but he's been a very steady hand on the tiller, and I am a great admirer and an advocate of his policies and programs.

"Anyone who can say, 'irrational exuberance' and screw up the market is someone you have to be really careful of. I wouldn't say he's personally popular. But he influenced the interest rate and that, in general, is one of the largest single factors behind the expansion."

—W. JAMES FARRELL,
CEO OF ILLINOIS TOOL WORKS INC.;
*CHICAGO TRIBUNE*, MAY 5, 1998

"If commerce rules the world, then Alan Greenspan is its king. This economist with the face of a basset hound has the amazing ability to yank the stock market in either direction with his abstruse remarks. More than the White House or Congress, the chairman of the Federal Reserve Bank may be responsible for this country's golden economy that has held off the dueling devils of unemployment and inflation."

—"GREENSPAN'S GOALS," EDITORIAL,
*THE SAN FRANCISCO CHRONICLE*,
SEPTEMBER 26, 1998

"It was his usual exercise in on-the-one-hand-this and on-the-other-hand-this," adding that the problem is that people tend to focus on just one 'hand.'

"The whole idea is that Fedspeak is an art form. There must be secret training sessions at the Fed called 'The Art of Obfuscation.'"

—PHILIP BRAVERMAN,
CHIEF ECONOMIST OF DKB SECURITIES CORP.,
AFTER GREENSPAN'S SPEECH AT THE
1997 HASKINS PARTNERS DINNER OF THE
STERN SCHOOL OF BUSINESS, NEW YORK UNIVERSITY,
NEW YORK CITY; MAY 8, 1997

"One of Greenspan's major legacies will be to make monetary policy more transparent."

—DAVID JONES, CHIEF ECONOMIST AT AUBREY G. LANSTON,
A WALL STREET DEALER IN U. S TREASURY ISSUES,
*THE NEWS AND OBSERVER* (RALEIGH, NC); MAY 10, 1997

"Greenspan is willing to try this experiment of low unemployment and low inflation right before our eyes."

—ELLIOTT PLAT, DIRECTOR OF ECONOMIC RESEARCH AT STOCK BROKERAGE
DONALDSON, LUFKIN, AND JENRETTE IN NEW YORK;
*FINANCIAL TIMES*, JULY 24, 1997

"The man is a bit like the Wizard of Oz. He has an incredible capacity for absorbing and interpreting data.

"Like any system that depends on an individual—monarchy, if you like—it's highly risky. If you could clone Greenspan and all his knowledge, then maybe it would be fine. But as I get older, I am more sympathetic to a gold standard kind of system than I used to be. Probably not literally a gold standard, but something more mechanical."

—CHARLES NELSON, PROFESSOR OF ECONOMICS AT THE UNIVERSITY OF
WASHINGTON AND A LONGTIME FED WATCHER, QUOTED BY BRUCE RAMSEY,
P-I COLUMNIST; *SEATTLE POST-INTELLIGENCER*, AUGUST 13, 1997

"The credibility of the Federal Reserve has never been higher, but too much of it rests upon the shoulders of one person. What happens when Mr. Greenspan goes or, heaven forbid, makes a serious policy error? If market confidence in his ability is shaken, the punishment will be harsh. To crown his achievements, one hopes that the Fed Reserve chairman would now concentrate on helping his colleagues raise their profile in the markets so that the Fed may continue to lead rather than be led by the markets after his retirement."

—MICHAEL NAAMEH, INVESTMENT DIRECTOR, CROWN AGENTS ASSET MANAGEMENT, LONDON; LETTERS TO THE EDITOR, *FINANCIAL TIMES* (LONDON), AUGUST 14, 1997

"If Alan Greenspan knows anything, he knows that he doesn't know everything, and he also knows that his words will be treated as if he were Moses coming down off the mountaintop after a visit with God."

—EDITORIAL, *DENVER ROCKY MOUNTAIN NEWS,* OCTOBER 10, 1997

• • •

On Alan Greenspan's nomination in 2000 to his fourth term as Fed chairman, as reported by various news media:

"I feel a key player in this period of economic prosperity has been Federal Reserve Board Chairman Alan Greenspan. I am confident that Chairman Greenspan's technical experience, common sense, and commitment to fiscal discipline will continue to expand our nation's prosperity for all Americans."

—VICE PRESIDENT AL GORE

"He's a nice man but I would prefer new and different leadership at the Fed."

—SEN. BYRON DORGAN, D–NORTH DAKOTA

"The president has made a wise and timely decision. It underscores that the country has been well served by an independent, nonpartisan Federal Reserve."
—REP. JAMES A. LEACH, R–IOWA, CHAIRMAN OF THE HOUSE BANKING AND
FINANCIAL SERVICES COMMITTEE

"There's a basic rule in business: Don't mess with success. That's why the reappointment of Alan Greenspan is such welcome news. Chairman Greenspan has provided thoughtful, forward-looking and very prudent leadership as head of the Federal Reserve, and his continued stewardship of the nation's monetary system bodes well for continued non-inflationary economic growth."
—JERRY JASINOWSKI, PRESIDENT OF THE NATIONAL
ASSOCIATION OF MANUFACTURERS

"His relentless pursuit of price stability is one of the key factors behind the robust economic growth we are experiencing today. Since Alan Greenspan has chaired the Federal Reserve, inflation and unemployment are both down nearly 2 percentage points, interest rates are down 2.5 percentage points, the Dow is up 325 percent and the economy has grown at a 3.2 percent annual rate."
—SEN. CONNIE MACK, R–FLORIDA, CHAIRMAN OF THE
JOINT ECONOMIC COMMITTEE

"The chairman, more than any other single individual, has aided in reducing unemployment and inflation at the same time for over seven years, a feat unheard of in many circles until his tenure. The Fed's chief duty is price stability and inflation control. Alan Greenspan has done that and done it well."
—REP. JIM SAXTON, R–NEW JERSEY, VICE CHAIRMAN OF THE
JOINT ECONOMIC COMMITTEE

"I strongly support the reappointment of Alan Greenspan. He's been good for the markets and instrumental in helping resolve the Asian financial crisis."

—DEMOCRATIC PRESIDENTIAL CANDIDATE BILL BRADLEY

(Interestingly enough, Bradley was one of only two dissenting votes in Greenspan's first nomination as Fed chief. At the time he said: "I believe we need a chairman with wider international experience at this time. My personal preference would have been for the administration to prevail upon Chairman Volcker to stay on for another term." )

"He has inspired confidence, and with good reason. His decisions have helped us to work toward a period of sustained economic growth."

—PRESIDENT BILL CLINTON

"Here in this country, Chairman Greenspan will bring all his skill to bear upon the task of promoting our continued economic growth while keeping inflation low. This is a point that's important to note: today, keeping down inflation and sustaining economic growth is not an either-or proposition; today, low inflation and economic growth can, and must, go hand in hand. Abroad, Chairman Greenspan will play an important role in seeking solutions to the problems of the developing countries and the massive debt some of them have accumulated.

"He'll work to insure an open and fair trading system among all nations, and he will be deeply involved in the restructuring and modernization of the American banking system, to keep our own capital markets competitive with others around the world."

—PRESIDENT RONALD REAGAN, ON GREENSPAN'S APPOINTMENT AS FED CHAIRMAN; AUGUST 11, 1987

• • •

In the 1950s, Saul Klaman, now vice chairman of Golembe Associates in Boston, met Alan Greenspan. Greenspan, a young economist, was working on a magazine article and went to Klaman, asking for data. "It doesn't exist," Klaman told him confidently. Greenspan thanked him and left.

When the magazine article appeared, color graphs and charts displayed the "nonexistent" information on housing.

"I was shocked," Klaman said. "I still don't know where the hell he got it. But I figured someone who was that inventive would go far."
—SAUL KLAMAN, QUOTED IN THE *ST. PETERSBURG TIMES*, JULY 26, 1987

"You wouldn't want Alan Greenspan to write the instructions for assembling a beach chair."
—ROBERT ORBEN, FORMER GERALD FORD SPEECHWRITER,
*MANCHESTER GUARDIAN WEEKLY*, DECEMBER 27, 1996

• • •

Greenspan's words have different meanings to different people. Here is a series of newspaper headlines that appeared after his testimony to Congress on June 7, 1995.

"Greenspan Sees Chance of Recession,"
*The New York Times*

"Recession Is Unlikely, Greenspan Concludes,"
*The Washington Post*

"Recession Risk Up, Greenspan Says," *Baltimore Sun*

"Fed Chairman Doesn't See Recession on the Horizon," *The Wall Street Journal*

• • •

It happened again two weeks later, after Greenspan spoke at the Economic Club of New York on June 20, 1995.

"Greenspan Predicts 'Modest' Recession,"
*The Idaho Statesman*

"Greenspan: Little Risk of Recession," *USA Today*

"Greenspan Hints at Interest Rate Cut,"
*Nashville Banner*

"Interest Rate Cut Not on Horizon, Greenspan Hints," *Los Angeles Daily News*

"Greenspan Hints Fed May Cut Interest Rates,"
*The Washington Post*

"Greenspan: Uncertainty Abounds,"
*The (Manchester, N.H.) Union Leader*

• • •

"Sometimes you just want to say, 'Damn it, Alan, tell me a dirty joke, or at least listen to one.'"
—ROBERT KAVESH, A FRIEND AND ECONOMICS PROFESSOR AT NEW YORK UNIVERSITY, *THE NEW YORK TIMES*, JUNE 3, 1987

"When Greenspan dies his headstone could read: 'I am guardedly optimistic about the next world, but remain cognizant of the downside risk.'"
—ECONOMIST JEREMY GLUCK,
*MANCHESTER GUARDIAN WEEKLY*, DECEMBER 27, 1996

# Index

# About the Author

L arry Kahaner is an award-winning journalist, author, lec turer, and licensed private investigator. He is the author of eight nonfiction books, including the best-selling *Competitive Intelligence,* considered a groundbreaking work in the field of business intelligence. The book has been translated into six languages and is a Book-of-the-Month Club alternative.

He has been a consultant for *Fortune* 500 companies including AT&T, MCIWorldcom, Monsanto, and Cable & Wireless, and scores of smaller and mid-sized companies and organizations, including Adler & Robin Books and the Gold Institute.

Kahaner is also the co-author of *Say It and Live It: The 50 Corporate Mission Statements That Hit the Mark* and author of *On the Line: The Men of MCI Who Took on AT&T and Won.* He is a former Washington staff correspondent for *Business Week* magazine, a reporter for Knight-Ridder newspapers, and founding editor of *Communications Daily.* He has written for many other publications, including *The Washington Post, The International Herald Tribune, The European,* and *The Christian Science Monitor.* He has appeared on CNN's *Larry King Live!;* CNBC's *Management Today; Evening Magazine;* National Public Radio's *All Things Considered; CBS Evening News;* the G. Gordon Liddy Show; the Derek McGinty Show

Voice of America's *Talk to America;* Fox TV News; Bloomberg Business News; and local TV and radio stations throughout North America.

He has presented before the Society of Competitive Intelligence Professionals Annual Conference; International Quality & Productivity Center, National Military Intelligence Association; American Recover Association Annual Meeting; Institute of Police Technology and Management; District of Columbia Police Academy; Halton Regional Police Department, Toronto, Canada; the Graduate Management School of the University of Indonesia in Jakarta, and dozens of colleges and universities.

Kahaner is a member of the Society of Competitive Intelligence Professionals, American Society of Industrial Security, Mystery Writers of America, and the Author's Guild. He is founder and president of McLean, Virginia–based KANE Associates International, Inc., a firm that specializes in intelligence matters for corporate clients.

His Web site is *www.kahaner.com.*

LTCM - Pg 45

Pg 90 Forecasting - Barbora Walters

I invested 15,000 and made $5000
What is the %

$$\frac{5000}{15,000} = 33\%$$